Simply The Best

Good Honest Cooking

Annabelle White
Kathy Paterson

NEW HOLLAND

Happy Cooking

Kathy

First published in 1999 by New Holland Publishers (NZ) Ltd
Auckland • Sydney • London • Cape Town

218 Lake Road, Northcote, Auckland, New Zealand
14 Aquatic Drive, Frenchs Forest, NSW 2086, Australia
24 Nutford Place, London W1H 6DQ, United Kingdom
80 McKenzie Street, Cape Town 8001, South Africa

Copyright © 1999 in text: Annabelle White and Kathy Paterson
Copyright © 1999 in photography: Kieran Scott
Copyright © 1999 New Holland Publishers (NZ) Ltd

ISBN: 1 877246 02 6

Publishing Manager: **Belinda Cooke**
Managing Editor: **Renée Lang**
Editor: **Margaret Sinclair**
Designer: **Sue Attwood**
Photographer: **Kieran Scott**
Printed through Bookbuilders, Hong Kong

Cover photograph: Shona's Pickled Plums

Contents

About the Authors

Annabelle White

Well-known as the fun and bubbly food editor for the *Sunday Star-Times*, Annabelle enjoys communicating about food. She always believes fresh, simple, seasonal food should be celebrated – and she has used this principle in her work as a radio broadcaster, food editor for *NZ House & Garden*, diplomatic caterer in Washington DC and as an avid traveller. She is a former secondary school teacher with an MA (Hons) in History and Geography. She admits her favourite food is roast chicken and a freshly laid boiled egg with salt and pepper.

Annabelle White

Kathy Paterson

Kathy Paterson

When Kathy was a toddler she spent hours sitting on the kitchen bench watching her mother baking, cooking and preserving. By the age of eight she was making cakes and biscuits. After completing the Cordon Bleu in Auckland she was invited back to teach both in Auckland and London.

After three years teaching she started catering and working at Austin's Cooking School in Auckland. From food styling for television and magazines to her busy catering business, Kathy enjoys the delicious diversity of her work. A self-confessed foodie, she admits her favourite food is fish and loves her mother's stewed fruit, custard and cream.

To our parents, with much love and affection.
We couldn't have done this without you …

John and Jacqueline White
Jim and Beverley Paterson

Introduction

If you can call a fellow foodie at 11pm to ask them
why your just-baked soufflé cake hasn't risen or
how you can prepare grilled prawn kebabs for a
hundred people (without an oven or a barbecue),
you know you have a true friend ...

Such is my friendship with Kathy Paterson. I met Kathy years ago at a luncheon she catered at Villa Maria Wines in Auckland. It had been a superb meal, amazing wines and good company. The flavours were tantalizing, the execution professional and the simplicity of the fresh, simple food, a delight. To this day, I remember the menu.

Over the years we have shared recipes, styled food together, organized functions and given each other support and inspiration for menus and helped solve problems. Producing this cookbook was a natural extension of our good times together. We are both very serious about good, simple recipes that can be easily achieved by the home cook. Forget complicated procedures, it is our aim to encourage joy, fun and confidence in the kitchen–not frustration and disappointment.

One of our favourite activities is to sit in each other's kitchens and – over copious cups of tea and coffee – talk food, recipes, fresh produce and new ingredients. We always end up cooking and have found the sharing of knowledge makes the long hours associated with our work easier and more fun.

While my background is more with culinary reference books and history texts, pen and notebook, chalk and computers, Kathy's background is that of a Cordon Bleu teacher and top caterer – but we both love sharing our love of food.

This book is a cherished collection of our favourite recipes. You will love these dishes – so put on that apron and join us in the kitchen. We promise you will be delighted with the results!

PS: Don't lend this book to anyone – you will never see it again. This is a gem.

Annabelle White

Annabelle White • Birkenhead Point

As usual Annabelle has left me very little to say.
That's the real bonus with keen foodies –
they can usually talk as well as they can cook and eat.

Kathy Paterson

Kathy Paterson • Mt Eden

Baking

Baking is a a proud tradition. Some of our happiest childhood memories are associated with the rustling of cake tins and the clinking of tea cups. In the past 'filling the tins' was a domestic duty; buying biscuits was seen as an extravagance. Today we have less time in the kitchen, but baking a cake or whipping up a batch of muffins brings hospitality and kindness to the fore.

Sauterne Grape Cake

When testing this recipe, we enjoyed it plain without the syrup – but the original recipe from Clearwater Winery in Hawke's Bay, New Zealand, has the syrup as a topping. We opted to pour half a cup of sauterne over the cake as soon as it came out of the oven.

300 g seedless fresh grapes
200 g butter
1 cup caster sugar
2 large eggs, lightly beaten
1 teaspoon vanilla essence
$^1/_3$ cup sauterne
3 cups flour
1 teaspoon baking powder

SYRUP:
$^1/_2$ cup white sugar
50 ml (or just under
    $^1/_4$ cup) water
sauterne
fresh grapes

Slice the grapes in half and place in a large mixing bowl. Melt the butter and add to the grapes. Add the sugar, beaten eggs, vanilla essence and sauterne. Mix in sifted flour and baking powder. Pour into a 22 cm tin lined with baking or butter paper. Bake at 180°C for 40–50 minutes or until golden brown.

Syrup: Place the sugar and water in a pot and bring to a hard boil until a syrup has formed. Add the sauterne to taste and the cut grapes.

....

NOTE: This cake looks magnificent resting on grape leaves on a platter, with a light dusting of icing sugar over the cake.

Rhubarb Sour Cream Cake

This cake is particularly delicious with morning coffee. If you want to feed extra cake-lovers you can double the recipe.

125 g butter
$1^1/_2$ cups brown sugar
2 large eggs
1 cup wholemeal flour
1 cup standard flour
1 teaspoon baking soda
1 teaspoon baking powder
$^1/_2$ teaspoon salt
1 cup sour cream
$1^1/_2$ cups rhubarb, cut into 1 cm pieces
$^1/_2$ cup chopped walnuts or pecans

GLAZE:
60 g butter
$^1/_2$ cup sugar
$^1/_2$ cup cream
$^1/_2$ teaspoon vanilla

Cream together the butter, brown sugar and eggs until light and fluffy. Combine the flours, baking soda, baking powder and salt. Add to the creamed mixture alternately with the sour cream, mixing well after each addition. Stir in the rhubarb and the nuts.

Spoon into a well-buttered 20 cm cake tin. Bake at 180°C for 45–50 minutes. Dust with icing sugar or top with this delicious glaze.

Glaze: Combine the butter, sugar, cream and vanilla in a small saucepan. Heat until the butter melts, then pour over the cooled cake.

....

NOTE: Remember when you double this recipe you will need a larger cake tin and you will also need to allow extra time for baking. Our large cake baked at 170°C for 80 minutes. We placed tin foil over the cake to prevent excessive browning in the last 30–40 minutes. Try to avoid using the fan bake for cakes, as it dries them – far better to use your regular bake function.

Mango Coconut Loaf

2 cups flour
2 teaspoons baking soda
2 teaspoons cinnamon
$^1/_2$ teaspoon salt
125 g butter

1 cup caster sugar
3 large eggs
$^1/_2$ cup vegetable oil
1 large ripe mango,
    peeled and chopped
1 cup coconut
$^1/_2$ cup raisins

Preheat the oven to 180°C. Butter a large loaf pan (30 cm x 15 cm x 8 cm) well. In a bowl, sift the flour, baking soda, cinnamon and salt.

In another bowl, cream the butter and the sugar until light. Add the eggs, one at a time, and the oil, then beat the mixture until combined well. Add the mango, coconut and raisins then gently fold in the dry ingredients in several batches. Do not overmix.

Place the batter in the baking tin and smooth the top. Bake for 50–60 minutes or until a skewer comes out clean. Let the loaf cool in the pan for 10 minutes then invert onto a rack to cool completely.

....

NOTE: If fresh mangoes are not available then drain a 425 g can of mangoes and dice the tinned fruit.

Coconut Pound Cake

This coconut cake is the perfect base for fresh berries and glazed plums. It keeps well and is a very versatile cake.

250 g butter, softened
2 cups sugar
5 large eggs
3 cups flour
$^1/_4$ teaspoon salt
2 teaspoons baking powder
1 cup milk
$1^1/_2$ cups coconut
1 teaspoon lemon juice
$^1/_2$ teaspoon vanilla

Cream the butter and sugar together until fluffy. Add the eggs one at a time, beating well after each addition.

Sift the flour with the salt and baking powder. Add alternately with milk to the creamed mixture, beating after each addition. Add coconut, lemon juice and vanilla.

Turn into a greased and floured 26 cm cake tin and bake at 160°C for 1 hour 20 minutes. Cool for 10 minutes, then remove from the pan and cool on a rack.

....

NOTE: Serve a slice of pound cake with crème fraiche and poached or grilled fruits.

Anzac Biscuits

Warning! These biscuits will become a family favourite. We found them to be so popular they disappeared as soon as they were made. The original recipe comes from the bubbly foodie, Pauline McKinlay, at Everyday Gourmet in Dunedin, New Zealand. Everyone loves Anzac biscuits, so wrap a few in cellophane and give them away as a present.

2 cups rolled oats
2 cups coconut
90 g or $^2/_3$ cup dried peaches, finely sliced
90 g or $^2/_3$ cup dried apricots, finely sliced
$^1/_2$ cup raisins
2 cups flour
1 cup raw sugar
$^3/_4$ cup lightly toasted
   sunflower seeds
285 g butter
$^2/_3$ cup golden syrup
2 teaspoons baking soda
4 tablespoons boiling water

Mix all the dry ingredients in a large roasting pan. It is a messy mix, so allow plenty of room.

Melt the butter and golden syrup together till just boiling. Blend the soda with the boiling water. Stir to dissolve. Remove the butter from the heat, add the soda and water mix and blend into the dry ingredients. Mix really well – a big, sturdy spoon works well. Squeeze, push and pull the dough in your hand so you achieve an even texture. Remember to compress the dough so an even biscuit will be produced that will not crack or crumble when baking.

Place 7.5 cm biscuits on ungreased baking trays and bake at 180°C for 20 minutes. If you have a fan bake oven, cook two trays at once and reduce your cooking time slightly.

These biscuits keep well in an airtight tin.

....

NOTE: You can dip these biscuits in warmed chocolate for an extra indulgence! Melt dark cooking chocolate in the microwave and smear the cooled biscuits with the chocolate.

Luxury Chocolate Chip Biscuits

This recipe has been adapted from cookies sold at the prestigious Neiman Marcus department store in the United States. Make tiny biscuits and serve them with coffee as a great after-dinner treat or wrap them in cellophane, tie a big ribbon around them, and give them to a friend as a great present!

$2^1/_2$ cups rolled oats
250 g butter
1 cup brown sugar
2 large eggs

1 teaspoon vanilla
2 cups flour
$^1/_2$ teaspoon salt
1 teaspoon baking powder
1 teaspoon soda
2 cups chocolate chips
125 g grated cooking
   chocolate
$1^1/_2$ cups chopped nuts

Measure the rolled oats and blend in the blender or food processor to a fine oatmeal powder.

Cream the butter and sugar. Add the eggs and vanilla. Mix together with the flour, oatmeal, salt, baking powder and soda. Add the chocolate chips, grated chocolate and nuts. Roll into balls, press down and place 5 cm apart on a baking sheet. Bake two trays at a time for 10–15 minutes on fan bake at 190°C, or 15–20 minutes at 190°C in a regular oven.

Anzac Biscuits

Fresh Asparagus and Bacon Toasted Roll-ups

I can hardly wait for fresh asparagus to come onto the market so I can make these. The bacon gives a wonderful burst of flavour. **KP**

4 rashers bacon, diced
250 g or 1 cup cream cheese, softened
freshly ground black pepper
16 thin slices white or light wholemeal sandwich bread
16 fresh asparagus spears, blanched
3 tablespoons melted butter

Cook the bacon till crisp. Combine the cream cheese, bacon and black pepper. Cut the crusts off the bread and flatten the bread using a rolling pin. Smear with the cream cheese mixture. Place the asparagus at one end of the bread and roll up. Trim the asparagus if necessary. Brush all sides with melted butter and place on an oven tray lined with baking paper. Place under a hot grill and cook until golden and crisp (about 5–10 minutes), turning them over to ensure an even colour. Serve hot.

NOTE: To blanch asparagus – just snap off the end of the asparagus, wash well and then plunge into boiling salted water for 20–30 seconds. Drain quickly, rinse under the cold tap and lay the asparagus on kitchen towel to dry off.

Cottage Cheese Bread

This bread is made daily in my kitchen, as it's so versatile. It does not keep well, but freezes and makes the best breadcrumbs. I make the dough into individual small loaves and slice them to make little open sandwiches with toppings like rare beef with a wholegrain mustard or smoked salmon with sour cream and a sprig of chervil. **KP**

Makes 8 small loaves

3 teaspoons dry yeast
$1/2$ teaspoon sugar
$1/4$ cup warm water

$2^1/2$–3 cups bread flour or high grade flour
1 teaspoon salt
$1/4$ teaspoon baking soda
1 egg
2 tablespoons butter, melted
250 g tub cottage cheese

In a small bowl put together the yeast, sugar and water – allow to froth for 5 minutes.

TO MAKE THE DOUGH:
Use a food processor or a mixer fitted with a dough hook. Sift the flour, salt and baking soda into the bowl. Add the egg, melted butter and cottage cheese with the yeast mixture. Knead until the dough is smooth and shiny. This will take about 5 minutes (10 minutes if kneading by hand). This is a very soft and moist dough. If dry, add more warm water during kneading.

On a floured benchtop, cut the dough into eight portions. Knead and shape into little loaves and place into greased baby loaf tins about 11 cm x 6.5 cm x 4 cm. Cover with oiled plastic wrap. Allow the dough to rise to the top of each tin then bake at 200°C for 10 minutes or until well browned. Remove the loaves from the tins and allow to cool. Each loaf will cut into six slices or you can leave them whole.

Moira's Coconut Cinnamon Loaf

When Moira makes this loaf the whole neighbourhood benefits. The aroma of cinnamon and coconut baking in the oven is just divine! **AW**

2 large eggs

$^1/_4$ cup oil (not olive)

1 cup sugar

250 g sour cream

$1^1/_2$ cups flour

$1^1/_2$ teaspoons baking powder

1 teaspoon baking soda

$^1/_4$ teaspoon salt

CINNAMON MIX:

$^1/_2$ cup coconut

$^1/_4$ cup brown sugar

2 teaspoons cinnamon

Mix the eggs until they are frothy. Beat in the oil and sugar, then add the sour cream and other ingredients. Grease a large loaf tin and place half the batter into it. Sprinkle half the cinnamon mixture over the batter. Add the remaining batter and sprinkle the rest of the cinnamon mix on top. Cut through the mixture with a knife for a marbling effect. Bake at 180°C for 55–60 minutes. Let the loaf stand for 10 minutes, then turn out.

NOTE: This loaf is a great contribution for a lunch or picnic. It is superb with morning coffee, served warm, fresh from the oven – though it is harder to cut. No icing or buttering is needed.

Morning Glory Muffins

$2^1/_2$ cups sugar

4 cups flour

4 teaspoons cinnamon

4 teaspoons baking soda

1 teaspoon salt

1 cup raisins, plumped in brandy and drained

1 cup coconut

4 cups grated carrots

2 cups grated apples

1 cup pecans or walnuts, roughly chopped

6 eggs

2 cups vegetable oil

1 teaspoon vanilla

Sift the dry ingredients into a large bowl. Lightly dust the raisins with flour and add to the dry ingredients with the coconut, carrots, apples and nuts. Stir well. Combine the eggs, oil and vanilla and add to the mix. Stir until just combined. Spoon the batter into large, deep, greased muffin pans and bake at 190°C for 25 minutes.

NOTE: This mixture makes 36 large muffins. You can halve the recipe if desired.

JUSTIN & TRACE

ADVOCATES FOR YOUR SUCCESS

Apricot Fudge

This very simple but stunning fudge is a recipe from an old school friend, Sue Nathan. I make this fudge most weeks and Annabelle only lets me in the front door if I have a few pieces of it with me.   **KP**

200 g unsalted butter
397 g can sweetened condensed milk
2 x 250 g packets round wine biscuits, crushed
2 cups dried apricots, chopped

ORANGE ICING:
3 cups icing sugar
grated rind and juice of 1 orange

Melt the butter in a large saucepan, then add the condensed milk. Stir in the crushed wine biscuits and the dried apricots. Press into a swiss roll tin lined with baking paper. Cover with plastic wrap and refrigerate overnight. Ice with orange icing.

Orange Icing: Mix the icing sugar, orange rind and juice together, adding more juice if necessary. Spread thinly over the fudge.

Cooked Coffee Fudge Slice

This recipe is from Jo Meredith, another old school friend. Years ago, we were working together at a stud farm and when not making this fudge we would boil up the can of condensed milk to make caramel – yum!   **KP**

225 g unsalted butter
2 x 397 g cans sweetened condensed milk
2 teaspoons golden syrup
2 cups good quality walnuts, chopped
2 x 250 g packets vanilla wine biscuits, crushed

COFFEE ICING:
3 cups icing sugar
1 tablespoon coffee essence
boiling water to mix

Melt the butter in a large saucepan. Beat in the condensed milk and golden syrup, then the chopped walnuts and crushed biscuits. Place the mixture into a swiss roll tin lined with baking paper, and bake at 170°C for 25–30 minutes. The slice should be golden brown on top and slightly soft to the touch. Remove from the oven and cool in the tin. Once cold, ice with coffee icing and, if wished, a few extra walnuts may be sprinkled on top.

Coffee Icing: Mix the ingredients together and spread evenly over the fudge.

'I make this fudge most weeks and Annabelle only lets me in the front door if I have a few pieces of it with me.'

Kathy

Chocolate Nutty Slab

This is a lovely, rich slice – a perfect finale to a good meal. Serve it with coffee, when you do not want to serve a dessert. **AW**

250 g butter

200 g dark chocolate

4 eggs

2 cups sugar

2 teaspoons vanilla

1 cup flour

$^1/_4$ teaspoon salt

2 cups walnuts, chopped

Melt the butter and chocolate in the microwave in 1-minute bursts on medium-low, stirring after each minute, until it is melted.

Whip the eggs and sugar until pale and creamy. Add the butter and chocolate mixture plus the vanilla. Add the sifted dry ingredients and fold in with the walnuts. Bake in a greased, lined, 23 cm square cake tin for 25 minutes at 180°C or until the slice has set. Take care not to overcook.

Chocolate Christmas Log

I'm a self-confessed chocolate snob and use the best chocolate I can find. Callebaut chocolate and a Dutch cocoa are my choices, available from specialty food stores. The results make the search worthwhile. **KP**

125 g dark chocolate

4 tablespoons chopped almonds, toasted for a better flavour

1 tablespoon almond liqueur or brandy

2 tablespoons icing sugar

1 egg white, lightly beaten

cocoa for rolling

FILLING:

30 g unsalted butter

1 tablespoon icing sugar

1 egg yolk

2 tablespoons finely chopped glacé apricots (or cherries or other glacé fruits)

Grate the chocolate and mix with the chopped almonds. Add the almond liqueur, icing sugar and then the egg white. Blend until the mixture binds well. Form into a log shape on a piece of baking paper. Flatten to 30 cm x 10 cm. Spread the filling evenly in a strip along the log. Roll up as you would a sponge roll. Chill well. Before serving, roll in cocoa. Cut into slices to serve. This log softens quickly so keep it in the refrigerator.

Filling: Cream the butter and sugar, then add the egg yolk. Stir in the chopped glacé apricots.

....

NOTE: This is a very small quantity of filling, but the perfect amount for this log.

Lunch

A leisurely lunch – the very words have delightful associations. Forget the hurried weekday sandwich and take time to savour food slowly in a beautiful spot. Let the setting, company, food and wine all be pleasant and in harmony. In its simplicity, you will achieve perfection.

Thai-style Eye Fillet of Beef

During my cooking career I have been very fortunate to work alongside some incredibly talented people. One such person is Scott Ashton. Working together in Auckland at Austin's Cooking School for some years, we discovered and rediscovered some great recipes. This beef was one of Scott's favourites. **KP**

Serves 8

1.5 kg whole eye fillet
4 cloves garlic, crushed
4 teaspoons sugar
8 teaspoons soy sauce
8 teaspoons lemon juice
8 teaspoons fish sauce
4 spring onions, finely sliced
1 bulb lemon grass, finely sliced
4–6 red chillies, finely chopped
6 teaspoons chopped mint
4 teaspoons chopped parsley
4 teaspoons chopped coriander plus sprigs for garnish

Trim the eye fillet of any fat and sinew. Grill to medium-rare, approximately 15–20 minutes, or barbecue as a whole fillet.

Combine all the remaining ingredients in a screw-top jar and shake well.

Slice the beef thinly and arrange on a serving platter. Sprinkle over the dressing just before serving and garnish with sprigs of coriander.

....

NOTE: Mini poppadoms, available at Asian food stores, are a good accompaniment.

Balsamic Onion Bread

Imagine a lazy, languid summer afternoon with a chargrilled eye fillet, a variety of condiments, this bread and a luscious green salad – the good times should be this simple!

Serves 6

1 tablespoon or 3 teaspoons yeast
1 teaspoon sugar
4 tablespoons warm water
3 cups flour
1 teaspoon salt
$^3/_4$ cup warm water
2 large red onions, thinly sliced
2 tablespoons butter or oil
freshly ground pepper
1 tablespoon balsamic vinegar
olive oil
2 sprigs fresh rosemary
1 teaspoon brown sugar
$^1/_2$ teaspoon sea salt
extra virgin olive oil

Combine the yeast, sugar and warm water in a bowl and leave to foam – about 10 minutes.

Sift the flour and salt into a bowl. Mix in the yeast mixture and $^3/_4$ cup of warm water. Mix to a soft dough then turn out onto a floured benchtop and knead, using extra flour if necessary.

Oil a large bowl and place the dough in it, turning once. Cover the top with plastic wrap and let rise in a warm place until double in volume – about 1 hour.

Cook the onions very slowly in butter until they have completely wilted and are translucent, about 45 minutes. Season with freshly ground pepper. Add the balsamic vinegar and gently toss through.

Knock back the dough and knead for 1–2 minutes. Roll out into a long sausage shape (approximately 45 cm long) and then form it into a circle. Oil a baking tray (or use a teflon sheet or baking paper) and place the ring of dough on it. Spread the onions all over the dough. Break the rosemary into pieces and place on the dough intermittently. Scatter the sugar and the salt over the top. Let the bread rise while the oven heats up (about 15 minutes) and then bake at 200°C for 20–30 minutes, until golden in colour. Eat warm, drizzled with extra virgin olive oil.

Parsnip Tart

Our keen samplers raved about this savoury tart for days. Leftovers were quickly consumed and promises extracted for more samples in the next few weeks!

Serves 6

PASTRY:
3 cups flour
pinch of salt
250 g soft butter, not melted
iced water to mix

FILLING:
100 g butter, chopped
1/2 onion, finely chopped
1 kg parsnips (about 4) peeled and coarsely chopped
1 whole nutmeg, grated
2 cups thickened cream
salt

Pastry: Mix the flour, salt and butter together to combine. Slowly add water to form a pastry ball. Wrap in plastic wrap and rest in the fridge for at least 30 minutes prior to making the tart. When ready to prepare the tart, place pastry in a greased 23 cm flan tin. Cover the tin with plastic wrap and place back in the fridge to rest again to avoid shrinkage when cooking.

Filling: Preheat the oven to 150°C. Melt the butter in a deep saucepan, add the onion and cook over a low heat until soft. Add the parsnip and cook over a medium heat until beginning to brown. Stir in nutmeg and cream, season to taste with salt and simmer for about 20 minutes or until the parsnip is soft and the cream is slightly thickened. Using a potato masher, mash the parsnip well, spoon into the pastry case and bake for about 35 minutes.

Serve a wedge of parsnip tart with your favourite relish or chutney and top with rocket leaves tossed in balsamic dressing.

NOTE: We did not bake the tart base before cooking. The pastry was uncooked when we filled it with the parsnip mixture. If you are in a hurry, buy commercial short crust pastry for this tart.

We used thickened cream for this recipe, but ordinary cream can also be used.

Harvest Pie

When making this pie, it is best to pre-cook the sturdy vegetables like pumpkin and broccoli in the microwave. This recipe delights everyone – it is a delicious celebration of vegetables! It is great hot or cold and is seasonally versatile. Serve with a crisp, green salad.

Serves 6

1 onion, chopped
1 large clove garlic, minced
2 tablespoons butter
500 g peeled pumpkin, par-cooked
60 g spinach
45 g broccoli, par-cooked
250 g crusty pie pastry
100 g blue cheese
2 eggs
1 cup cream
milk for pastry glazing

Sweat the onion and garlic in butter. Slice and pre-cook the chosen vegetables.

Roll out the pastry and place in a 28–30 cm ovenproof dish. Let the pastry fall over the sides of the pie plate for a rustic look. Place all the vegetables in the uncooked pie shell. Crumble the blue cheese over the vegetables. Beat the eggs and cream together, and pour over the cheese and vegetables.

Brush the pastry edges with milk. Bake in a moderate 180°C oven until golden. Allow 40 minutes.

NOTE: Additional vegetables you could use in this pie with success include thickly sliced leeks, bok choy or cauliflower.

This pie is delicious served with a spoonful of chutney or our delicious Tomato Kasundi (see page 58).

Feta Cheese Galette

Serves 6

1¹/₂ cups flour
pinch of salt
135 g butter, very cold
¹/₃ cup cold water
150 g feta cheese
120 g ricotta
90 g fresh mozzarella, grated
¹/₄ cup sour cream or crème fraiche
2 tablespoons grated Parmesan
salt and freshly ground black pepper

Place the flour and salt on a cold work surface. Dice the butter into 12 mm pieces. With a pastry scraper, cut the butter into the flour and salt until the butter is the size of peas. Add all of the water and mix until it forms a ball. Alternatively, this pastry can be made in an electric mixer using the same instructions. On a well-floured surface roll the dough into a 40 cm circle. Place in the fridge while you assemble the filling.

Mix together the feta cheese, ricotta, mozzarella, sour cream or crème fraiche and Parmesan. Mix well and season with salt and pepper. Remove the pastry from the fridge. Spread the cheese over the pastry leaving a 6 cm border uncovered. Fold the uncovered edge of the pastry over the cheese, pleating it to make it fit.

Fan bake at 190°C for 20 minutes until golden brown. Otherwise bake in a 180°C oven for 35–40 minutes. Remove from the oven. After 5 minutes, slide the galette off the oven dish and onto a cooling rack. Let it rest 5 minutes, then serve.

....

NOTE: Serve this delicious galette with a contrasting topping, for example, marinated chargrilled capsicum, and a salad with the peppery overtones of rocket and other salad greens – all topped with a tangy vinaigrette. The rich full flavour of the galette would also be complemented by a lemon powered vinaigrette.

Curried Parsnip Soup

Serves 4–6

1 large onion
3 cloves garlic
olive oil
1 tablespoon curry powder
6 medium parsnips, peeled and finely sliced
5¹/₂ cups chicken stock
salt and pepper to taste
fresh coriander, chopped and to garnish
¹/₂ cup coconut cream or cream

Cook the onion and the garlic in a little olive oil until soft. Add the curry powder and the peeled and finely sliced parsnips. Sweat for 5 minutes, making sure the parsnips do not catch, then add the chicken stock. Bring to the boil and simmer for 45 minutes. Adjust the seasonings. Purée, then add freshly chopped coriander and coconut cream or cream just prior to serving. Garnish with fresh coriander.

....

NOTE: If your family is not fond of coriander you can use parsley and/or chives to garnish and enhance this soup. You can also use low-fat milk instead of the cream, if you prefer.

Asian Gravadlax with Coriander and Lime Dressing

On a recent trip to London, I asked my good friend, Louise Adams, to give me two of her favourite recipes of the moment. This is one of her selection.   **KP**

Serves 10

GRAVADLAX:

2 side fillets salmon, skin on, boned

3 tablespoons sea salt

3 tablespoons white sugar

3 tablespoons peeled and grated root ginger

3 bulbs lemon grass,
    finely sliced

grated rind of 3 limes
    (or 2 lemons)

2 teaspoons black
    peppercorns, coarsely
    crushed

2 chillies, chopped

3 tablespoons chopped
    coriander leaves and
    root

CORIANDER AND LIME DRESSING:

2 egg yolks

2 teaspoons Dijon mustard

2 teaspoons caster sugar

1 cup oil

2.5 cm piece of root
    ginger, peeled and grated

juice of 1 lime

2 tablespoons coriander, chopped

salt and pepper to taste

4 tablespoons crème fraiche

Gravadlax: Mix all the above ingredients together except the salmon. Put quarter of this Asian mix into a flat china dish, and place one salmon fillet skin-side down onto it. Spread half of the Asian mix on the salmon and place the remaining fillet on top. Spread the last quarter of the Asian mix onto the skin of the top fillet. Cover with foil. Place a plate on top and some weights, eg, cans of food. Leave to marinate overnight. Using a very sharp knife, cut the salmon into very thin slices for serving.

Dressing: In a food processor whisk the egg yolks, Dijon mustard and sugar together. Drizzle in the oil slowly until thick. Add ginger, lime juice and coriander. Season to taste. Just before serving add crème fraiche.

....

NOTE: This is a very rich dish. Serve with a green salad or as a dish for a buffet.

Salmon and Caper Tartare

This is a super, simple, stunning starter created by Kathy. Whenever you eat this salmon you feel instantly revived.   **AW**

Serves 4

3 tablespoons salted capers

1 bunch spring onions or
    1 medium red onion

small bunch mint

500 g salmon fillets,
    skinned and boned

3 tablespoons vodka or gin

3 tablespoons extra virgin
    olive oil or lemon-infused
    olive oil

3 tablespoons lemon juice

salt and pepper

Soak the capers overnight in cold water, drain and rinse well. Finely chop the spring onions. Remove stalks from the mint and chop the leaves. Cut the salmon into small dice. Combine all ingredients and refrigerate overnight. Remove from the fridge 15–20 minutes before serving so the flavours can develop at room temperature. If desired, add more fresh mint before serving, for colour.

Salmon and Caper Tartare

American Picnic Pasta Salad

Serves 10–15

10 eggs
1 x 500 g packet pasta – use any interesting
    variety
2 tablespoons olive oil
1 head celery
2 bunches spring onions
2 cucumbers
black pepper
chopped fresh parsley
2 tablespoons wholegrain honey mustard
2 cups thick Lemon Mayonnaise

Boil the eggs for 8 minutes only. Peel, then place in cold water and reserve.

Cook the pasta in salted water according to packet instructions, or until al dente. Drain well, then pour over olive oil and toss. Add the celery and spring onions (cut into thin slices on the diagonal) and the cucumbers (skinned, seeded and cut into chunks). Mix the pepper, chopped parsley and mustard with the Lemon Mayonnaise, and fold into the pasta. Finally, dry and quarter the reserved eggs and gently mix them in, trying to avoid breaking them up.

Turn onto a serving platter and garnish with extra chopped parsley. If desired you can also add some chopped cooked bacon.

Lemon Mayonnaise

6 egg yolks
1 teaspoon Dijon mustard
500 ml mild olive oil
juice of 4 lemons, approximately
salt

Place yolks and mustard in a food processor fitted with a steel blade and process for 15 seconds. Remove the feed tube and, with the machine running, add the oil in a thin, steady stream. Add lemon juice as it becomes too thick. Season with salt. If it tastes a little oily, add more salt.

Green Herb Sauce

Ali Richardson and I taught at the Cordon Bleu School in Auckland. Some time ago she gave me this Herb Sauce recipe to go with hot or cold beef or chargrilled salmon fillets. Try it at your next buffet lunch.   **KP**

$1^1/_2$ cups parsley
1 bunch chives
$^1/_4$ cup salted capers (soaked overnight),
    washed and drained
3 cloves garlic, crushed
1 teaspoon Dijon mustard
2 eggs
1–2 cups olive oil
lemon juice
salt and pepper to taste

Using a food processor, process the parsley, chives, capers, garlic and mustard. Add the eggs, then drizzle in olive oil and some lemon juice until thick. Season with salt and pepper. Keeps well for one week in the refrigerator.

Creole Remoulade Sauce

There are lots of versions of a Remoulade Sauce. This is a simplified one, but it is still very good. Serve with chargrilled prawns, crumbed mussels, roast chicken or even corned beef!

$^1/_2$ cup thick Lemon Mayonnaise
2 sticks celery, finely chopped
4 spring onions, finely chopped
2 tablespoons chopped parsley
1 tablespoon wholegrain mustard
1 tablespoon tomato sauce
1 tablespoon Worcestershire sauce
4 cloves garlic, crushed
2 red chillies, finely chopped
1 teaspoon paprika
salt to taste

Make the mayonnaise (see the recipe for Lemon Mayonnaise, this page), then add all the remaining ingredients. Chill.

Cauliflower Cheese Pie

Serves 4

2 cups packed, grated potatoes
1 teaspoon salt
3 large eggs
$^1/_4$ cup grated onion
1 cup chopped onion
2 cloves garlic, minced
3 tablespoons butter
1 teaspoon dried thyme or 2–3 teaspoons fresh
pepper to taste
paprika to taste
1 teaspoon dried basil or 2–3 teaspoons fresh
$^1/_2$ cauliflower, broken into
    florets
$1^1/_2$ cups grated cheese
$^1/_4$ cup milk

Salt the grated potato with $^1/_2$ teaspoon salt. Let stand for 10 minutes, then squeeze out the excess water. Beat 1 egg and add to the potato along with the grated onion. Pat into a well-oiled pie plate and bake at 190°C for 30 minutes or until golden brown.

Cook the chopped onion and garlic in butter. Add the herbs and seasonings (including the other $^1/_2$ teaspoon salt) and cauliflower and cook for 10 minutes. Spread half the cheese in the pie plate, then the cauliflower mixture, then the remaining cheese. Beat together the two remaining eggs and milk and pour all over the pie. Bake at 190°C for 30–40 minutes or until set.

Chicken Mint Salad

Serves 2–4

2 cooked chicken breasts
50 g sugar snap peas
1 telegraph cucumber
3 spring onions
$^1/_4$ cup packed fresh mint leaves
1 teaspoon minced, peeled fresh ginger root
$1^1/_2$ tablespoons olive oil
$1^1/_2$ tablespoons fresh lemon juice
$^1/_2$ avocado

Discard the chicken skin and cut meat crosswise into 5 mm thick slices. Trim the peas. Halve the cucumber lengthways and seed. Cut the peas, cucumber and spring onions diagonally into thin slices and chop the mint. In a large bowl toss together all ingredients and season with salt and pepper.

'The most indispensable ingredient of
all good home cooking:
love for those you are cooking for.'

Sophia Loren

Lemon Tartlets

These Lemon Tartlets seem to have followed me. We used to serve them with coffee at all day cooking demonstrations in England, and then at Austins Catering in Auckland. **KP**

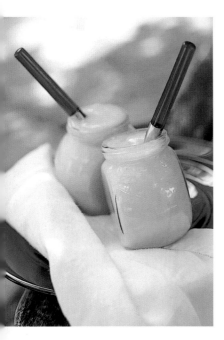

LEMON CURD FILLING:
170 g cup caster sugar
115 g unsalted butter
grated rind and juice of
   2 large lemons
3 eggs, lightly beaten

PASTRY:
225 g flour
115 g unsalted butter,
   softened
115 g caster sugar
4 egg yolks
2 drops vanilla essence

Lemon Curd Filling: Place the sugar, butter, rind and strained lemon juice into a heavy-based saucepan. Cook slowly until the sugar is dissolved and the butter melted. Sieve the eggs, using a plastic or stainless steel sieve, into the saucepan and stir well. Continue stirring and cook until the mixture is thick. Keep covered in the refrigerator or put into clean jars with tight-fitting lids.

Pastry: Sift the flour onto the benchtop. Make a well in the centre, and in this place the other ingredients. Using the fingertips of one hand, work only the butter, sugar, yolks and vanilla essence together. Then, once creamed, draw in the flour and knead lightly until smooth. Chill for 1 hour before using.

Assembly: Roll the pastry out thinly on a lightly floured benchtop. Using plain pastry cutters, cut out rounds to fill small tartlet tins. Press each pastry round into its tin and prick with a fork.

When using the smallest tartlet tins there is no need to bake blind (see page 46). Chill the pastry cases again before baking at 180°C until a pale biscuit colour, about 6 minutes. Cool. Fill with Lemon Curd just before serving.

The tartlets can be stored in an airtight container for up to one week.

....

NOTE: When making Lemon Curd – make a small amount like this, often, as it is best used within a week of being made. Store in the fridge.

Sieving the eggs is important to stop egg flecks appearing in the cooked mixture. Metal sieves (other than stainless steel) can impart an unpleasant flavour.

Celebrate a special occasion by having Lemon Curd and waffles for brunch. Try using Lemon Curd with whipped cream to garnish your favourite lemon cake, or mix it with whipped cream and passion fruit syrup (minus seeds) for a delicious addition to a fruit or fruit cake dessert. Lemon Curd in a dainty jar dressed up with a bow makes a great present – with a bottle of wine when going to a friend's home for dinner or as a special house-warming present.

Picnics

We have always wanted to set up a table for a picnic in a field of sunflowers. The seed heads sway in the breeze, the golden petals glow and the table is bathed in warm sunlight. Our food is portable and full-flavoured. Could this be paradise?

Bacon, Blue Cheese and Spinach Sandwich

125 g blue cheese
1 French baguette or bread stick
Blue Cheese Dressing (see below)
1 cup cooked and diced bacon
spinach leaves
6 thin strips red capsicum

Cut the blue cheese into wedges. Open the French bread and remove some of the bread filling. Spread the loaf with a coating of dressing and place the rest of the filling contents on top of the dressing. Extra dressing can be added when serving.

NOTE: This sandwich is also delicious if chicken and lettuce are used in place of the bacon and spinach.

Blue Cheese Dressing

This thick dressing is ideal for sandwiches.

100 g blue cheese
3 tablespoons sour cream
   or yoghurt
1 spring onion, finely diced
2 cloves garlic, crushed
2 tablespoons mayonnaise
3 tablespoons olive oil
1 tablespoon white wine vinegar
1 teaspoon Dijon mustard

Remove the rind from the blue cheese and cut into wedges. Put all the ingredients in a blender and mix until smooth. Season with pepper to taste and store in the fridge.

Salmon and Wasabi Wholegrain Sandwich

4 wholegrain rolls
12 small slices smoked salmon
salad greens
wasabi mayonnaise

Split the rolls and smear some of the wasabi mayonnaise onto them. Lay the smoked salmon on top, allowing three pieces of salmon per roll, and a little extra mayonnaise. Top with salad greens, wrap in plastic wrap and store in the picnic basket.

NOTE: To make wasabi mayonnaise when you are in a hurry – just combine ready-mix wasabi paste (available at your supermarket) with good quality commercial mayonnaise. The horse-radish flavour has a great affinity with salmon. Use a small amount at first, it is powerful stuff!

Salmon and Wasabi
Wholegrain Sandwich

Muffuletta

This is an Italian-style stuffed bread. Try to use good olives and oil, as it makes a big difference to the final result.

Serves 6–8

1 cup green olives, pitted
1 cup black olives, pitted
1/4 cup olive oil
1/4 cup chopped Italian
    parsley
2 capsicums, roasted,
    seeded, peeled and
    chopped
1 teaspoon fresh oregano,
    chopped
juice of 1 small lemon
freshly ground black
    pepper
1 round Italian loaf,
    approximately 25 cm
    in diameter
2 cups shredded lettuce
1 cup chopped tomatoes
225 g salami, thinly sliced
115 g tasty cheese, thinly sliced

In a bowl combine the olives, oil, parsley, capsicums, oregano, lemon juice and black pepper. Cover and refrigerate overnight.

Cut the bread horizontally and pull out most of the soft dough in the middle. Drain the olive salad and brush both pieces of bread with the marinade. Use it all. Place half of the olive salad in the hollow of one piece of bread. In layers, add half the lettuce, half the tomatoes, the salami, the cheese, then the remaining lettuce and tomatoes. Finally, put the rest of the olive salad on the other side of the loaf. Press the sides together and wrap in plastic wrap. Put the loaf in the refrigerator with a weight on top and leave at least 30 minutes. Cut into wedges for serving.

Spinach and Mushroom Roulade

Thank you to frozen spinach. It has made this recipe so quick. Italians are even more fortunate as all over Italy they can buy freshly cooked, drained spinach in their local supermarkets and delis.

Serves 4–6

1 tablespoon butter
1 packet (450–500 g) frozen spinach, thawed
    and drained
salt and pepper
4 eggs, separated
grated Parmesan

FILLING:
170 g mushrooms, wiped and thinly sliced
2 tablespoons butter
1 tablespoon flour
1/2 cup milk
3 tablespoons cream
1 whole nutmeg, grated
salt and black pepper

Melt the butter in a large saucepan, then add the spinach and toss over a high heat for about 1 minute to remove excess moisture. Add seasonings, then add 4 egg yolks, one at a time, beating well. Whip the egg whites until just holding their shape and fold into the spinach. Place mixture in a swiss roll tin lined with baking paper. Sprinkle with grated Parmesan and bake at 200°C for 10 minutes.

Remove cooked roulade from the oven. Turn out onto a sheet of baking paper sprinkled with Parmesan. Peel off the paper on which the roulade was cooked. Spread with the mushroom filling and roll up.

Filling: Slice the mushrooms and cook in half the butter until soft. Remove the mushrooms and set aside. Melt the remaining butter. Remove from the heat and add the flour. Pour on the milk and bring to the boil. Once thickened, add the cream and a dusting of grated nutmeg, salt and black pepper to taste. Stir in the mushrooms and any liquid that has formed.

**Spinach and
Mushroom Roulade**

Asian Chicken Roll

Take this chunky filling with you on a picnic and fill freshly baked bread rolls with this memorable flavour combination. Warning: it is highly addictive!

Serves 6–8

2 cups mirin or rice wine

2 tablespoons fish sauce

4 tablespoons soy sauce

4 tablespoons brown sugar

3 teaspoons finely grated ginger

2 teaspoons rice wine vinegar

4 teaspoons sweet chilli sauce

garlic to taste

1 finely chopped spring onion

1.5 kg boneless chicken thighs

Combine all the ingredients except the chicken and boil for 5 minutes. Cool and pour this marinade over the chicken pieces in a large resealable bag. Refrigerate overnight, then remove the chicken and bake or grill it. Serve warm or cold.

....

NOTE: Mirin and rice wine vinegar are available from Asian supply stores. You can dice the chicken into smaller pieces, if desired, or leave the thigh pieces whole. The smaller the pieces of chicken, the quicker the cooking time.

Clark's Tomato, Mozzarella and Basil Pesto Flan

No cookbook would be complete without a recipe from Julie Clark from Clark's in the Library in Wellington and Palmerston North. Julie is always inventive, always sharing and encouraging – and her food is inspirational. Try her treatment of tomatoes and basil in a flan!

Serves 6–8

1 x 23 cm flan tin lined with short pastry

9 tomatoes

250 g mozzarella

1 cup milk

2 large eggs

3 tablespoons basil pesto

salt and pepper to season

For this recipe use rolled commercial short savoury pastry. If it is not rolled, then leave it in the fridge for 20 minutes after rolling. All pastry responds well to a resting period in the fridge.

After resting, bake the flan blind (see below) at 200°C for 15 minutes. Let cool.

Layer the flan with thick slices of tomato and thick slices of mozzarella cheese. Slant the cheese and tomato slices so they overlap slightly. Pack them in tightly.

Place 1 cup of milk in a bowl and whisk in the eggs. Add the pesto and season well. Pour over the tomatoes and mozzarella. Bake at 180°C for 30 minutes or until the custard is firm.

....

NOTE: To bake blind is to put weights such as beans into the pastry shell and cover the shell with foil, before baking. The weights keep the base in shape while cooking and the foil prevents excessive browning.

Clark's Tomato, Mozzarella and Basil Pesto Flan

Nicola's Fish Cakes

Nicola has been part of the team creating this book and her fish cakes are legendary.

Serves 8–10

500 g boneless salmon

1 kg potatoes

1 teaspoon salt

2 tablespoons finely
 chopped dill or parsley

salt and pepper

3 cups fresh white
 breadcrumbs

3/4 cup flour

2 eggs

vegetable oil

Place salmon on an oven tray and cover with tin foil. Cook in the oven for 10 minutes at 180°C.

Peel and cut the potatoes. Put them into a saucepan, cover with cold water and add the salt. Boil the potatoes until cooked. When they are done, either mash them by hand or pass them through a sieve. For the best results it is important that there are no lumps. Add the cooked salmon and the herbs. Season to taste. Chill the mixture for at least an hour.

When the mixture has chilled, shape it into balls no bigger than a tennis ball. Put the breadcrumbs and flour into separate flat dishes. Lightly beat the eggs in a large bowl. Roll the fish balls in the flour, next cover with the egg and then roll in the breadcrumbs. Put the balls onto a flat board and use a spatula to flatten each ball into a cake about 2 cm high. Smooth the sides to get an even round shape.

To cook the fish cakes evenly, fill the frying pan about one-third full of oil. Heat the oil until it starts to sizzle when you drop some crumbs into it. Cook the fish cakes on medium heat and turn them over once to brown both sides. Serve with your favourite home-made tomato sauce or green salsa and salad.

Fresh Cucumber and Radish Relish

1 small cucumber, cut into fine strips
 (peeled if preferred)

3 radishes, cut into fine strips or slices

1/2 cup cream, whipped

1 cup plain unsweetened yoghurt

2 teaspoons fresh horse-radish, finely grated
 (or horse-radish cream if fresh not available)

1 tablespoon chopped fresh dill

salt and black pepper to taste

Prepare all ingredients separately and mix together just before serving for a picnic at the bottom of your garden, or place in a plastic container with a tight-fitting lid to take in a chilly bin for a picnic away from home. Delicious served with Nicola's Fish Cakes.

'The combination of these fish cakes and the relish is just divine. Picnics should always be this substantial.'

Annabelle

Fresh Cucumber
and Radish Relish with
Nicola's Fish Cakes

Simply Delicious and Easy Smoked Salmon Mousse

Serves 10

225 g smoked salmon
juice of 2–3 lemons
1 cup cream

Place smoked salmon and lemon juice into a food processor bowl and process briefly. Add half of the measured cream and process briefly again. Whip the remaining cream and fold through the salmon mixture. Season with a little salt if necessary. Chill before serving for at least 2 hours. Keep in your chilly bin.

Serve with rice crackers or crusty bread.

Fruit and Nut Tea Loaf

This loaf is a great Kiwi classic. Before the invasion of biscotti and florentines into coffee bars throughout the country, there was the ubiquitous tray of heavily buttered fruit loaf sitting proudly in the glass cabinets. Keep up the tradition on your next picnic.

1 cup sugar
1 cup water or cold tea
$^3/_4$ cup sultanas
1 tablespoon or 15 g butter
1 teaspoon baking soda
1 egg
pinch of salt
1 mashed banana
$^1/_2$ teaspoon nutmeg
$^1/_2$ teaspoon mixed spice or cinnamon
2 cups flour
2 teaspoons baking powder

Boil the sugar, water and sultanas for a few minutes until the fruit is plump. After you have reached boiling point, allow 5–10 minutes on a gentle simmer. Add the butter and allow the fruit to cool slightly, before adding the soda, beaten egg, salt, mashed banana and nutmeg and other spices. Lastly, add the sifted flour and baking powder.

Place the mix in a buttered loaf pan and bake at 180°C for 45–55 minutes. This will depend on the depth of your tin. Test after 45 minutes.

....

NOTE: This loaf slices easily if left for 24 hours before using. It is super-fast to make and very economical.

Glazed Chicken Roulade

Serves 8

8 boned and skinned chicken breasts
   with fillet
8 long rashers of bacon, rind removed
8 tablespoons plum sauce
oil

RICE STUFFING:
1 cup long grain white rice, cooked and cooled
3–4 tablespoons chopped parsley
1 egg, lightly beaten
salt and pepper

Make the rice stuffing by combining all the ingredients. Open out the chicken breasts and place some of the stuffing on each. Pull the fillet over, then roll up. Wrap a bacon rasher around each one to secure the stuffing inside the fillet. Brush 1 tablespoon of the plum sauce over each chicken roulade.

Place in a baking dish. Sprinkle over a little oil and bake at 190°C for 20–25 minutes. Cut each roulade into four slices before serving.

Chicken Drumsticks

Serves 4

3 cloves garlic, chopped
1 good-sized (about 5 cm) piece of root ginger,
   peeled and chopped
1 red chilli, chopped
1 bunch fresh coriander, well washed
8 chicken drumsticks
2 tablespoons olive oil
freshly ground black pepper
2 cups chicken stock
1 tablespoon Thai fish sauce

In a small bowl combine the garlic, ginger, chilli and the chopped coriander roots (keep the leaves). Marinate the chicken in 1 tablespoon of the measured oil and the garlic mixture. Grind over plenty of black pepper. Leave overnight in the refrigerator.

Pan-fry the chicken quickly in the remaining tablespoon of oil. Transfer to a roasting dish and pour over the stock. Cook at 190°C for 30 minutes or until the juices run clear. Add the fish sauce and adjust seasonings if necessary. Sprinkle over the coriander leaves.

'Cooked chicken is the perfect picnic fare.
Always popular, and easy to transport
and consume, it enjoys a happy
association with bold flavours.'

Annabelle

**Glazed Chicken Roulade
and Chicken Drumsticks**

Ginger Pear Streusel Cake

This recipe is another Julie Clark delight. Pears and ginger are a marriage made in heaven – like bacon and eggs or tomato and basil, some things should always be together!

CAKE:

3¼ cups flour

1 cup sugar

2 heaped teaspoons baking powder

¼ teaspoon salt

250 g butter, melted and cooled slightly

1½ teaspoons vanilla essence

4 large eggs

¼ cup milk

170 g crystallized ginger, finely chopped

5 pears, peeled, quartered and thinly sliced

GINGER STREUSEL:

¾ cup flour

½ cup brown sugar

5 teaspoons ground ginger

100 g butter, softened

Cake: Butter and lightly flour a 28 cm loose-bottomed cake tin. In a large bowl mix the flour, sugar, baking powder and salt. In another bowl mix the melted butter, vanilla essence, eggs and milk until well combined. Add the ginger and three of the pears to the flour mix and coat well. Don't worry if the pears break up.

Mix the wet mix (the eggs, milk etc) into the dry mix, as you do with muffins. Be very careful not to overmix – stir until the mixtures are just blended, that's all! Place the mixture in the cake tin and sprinkle half the streusel mixture over the batter. Cover the cake with the remaining two pears and top with the rest of the streusel. Bake at 180°C for 1 hour or until a skewer comes out clean.

Ginger Streusel: Combine the ingredients in a food processor and pulse until the mixture resembles breadcrumbs.

....

NOTE: If eating at home, cutting and serving this cake warm, with a mixture of half whipped cream and half plain yoghurt, is to be encouraged.

West Virginia Finest Butter Cookies

My mother, Jacqueline White, found this recipe in an obscure recipe book many years ago. Over time she has adapted it to make it her own. Whenever she makes these cookies everyone groans, as you are eating them for ages. This recipe will make around 76 cookies – so think presents for others! You will make more than you need for your family picnic.   **AW**

250 g butter

1 cup sugar

1 cup brown sugar

1 large egg

1 cup oil

1 cup rolled oats

1 cup corn flakes, crushed, or 1 cup crushed Weet-Bix

½ cup coconut

½ cup walnuts, chopped

3½ cups sifted flour

1 teaspoon soda

½ teaspoon salt

1 teaspoon vanilla

In a large mixing bowl, cream the butter and sugars until light and fluffy. Add egg and mix well. Then add the oil. Mix thoroughly. Add rolled oats, corn flakes, coconut and nuts. Stir well. Add the flour, soda, salt and vanilla. Mix well.

Form into balls, using a teaspoon, and place on an ungreased tray. Bake at 180°C for 18–20 minutes, or on fan bake at 180°C for 10–12 minutes. Allow to cool on the biscuit sheet for a few minutes before removing.

Dinner

Nothing delights quite like an invitation to dinner. An opportunity to share good news and concerns with friends and family, it soothes and recharges the soul. Add simple elegance, good wine and a menu celebrating fresh seasonal produce – you will wish your dinner could last all night.

Roast Chicken on Quinoa with Tomato Kasundi

Quinoa, a grain, was cultivated in the Andes by Inca farmers hundreds of years ago.

Serves 4

4 x 380 g baby chickens
salt and pepper
2 roughly chopped oranges
$1/2$ cup roughly sliced fresh ginger
1 cup warm water

QUINOA:
100 g butter
$1/2$ cup leek, finely diced
$1/2$ cup carrot, peeled and finely diced
1 cup quinoa grains
2 cups water

1 cup Tomato Kasundi

Preheat the oven to 230°C. Rinse out the cavity of the chickens, pat dry and lightly season with salt and pepper. Mix the orange and ginger together, then use the mix to stuff the chickens. Tie the legs together with string. Lightly season the outside of the chickens with salt and pepper. Place in a roasting tray and pour a cup of warm water into the tray. Place the chickens in the oven.

Baste with the cooking liquid after 10 minutes and turn the oven down to 180°C for approximately another 20 minutes or until the juices run clear when a chicken is tipped up.

While the chickens are cooking, prepare the quinoa. Melt 50 g butter in a medium-sized saucepan. When the butter begins to bubble add the leeks and carrots and cook for 2–3 minutes, stirring. Add another 50 g of butter and the quinoa. Cook for another 2–3 minutes then add 2 cups of water. Bring to the boil, cover with a lid and simmer gently for 15 minutes.

ASSEMBLY:
Reheat the quinoa if necessary and divide between four warm plates. Remove the string from the baby chickens, place on each plate and serve with Tomato Kasundi.

Tomato Kasundi

Kasundi is an Indian spicy chutney full of mustard seeds and with hints of garlic and ginger. Serve it with savoury pies, cold meats, barbecue fare or bread and crackers. When you become completely addicted, you will eat it by the spoonful direct from the pot.

Makes 3–5 large preserving jars

4–5 kg tomatoes
150 g salt
200 g cumin seeds
200 g coriander seeds
250 ml peanut oil
200 g yellow mustard seeds
100 g black mustard seeds
100 g fresh turmeric or 2 tablespoons
    turmeric powder
chilli to taste
300–450 g root ginger, grated
4 bulbs garlic
20 stems fresh curry leaves
800 g sugar
1.5 litres white wine vinegar

Chop the tomatoes coarsely and put in a large bowl. Sprinkle with salt, cover and set aside overnight.

Roast and grind the cumin and coriander seeds. Reserve.

Place some of the oil in a hot pan and cook all the mustard seeds gently until they pop.

In another large pan, heat $1/2$ cup of oil and cook the cumin and coriander seeds until fragrant. Add the popped mustard seeds and gently blend through.

Drain off the tomatoes and discard the juice (and any of the salt that is still obvious). Place in a large stock pot, with the mustard seed mix, and add the remaining ingredients. Simmer gently, uncovered, stirring frequently, for $1^1/2$ hours. Set aside to cool before pouring into clean, dry, glass jars. Store sealed in the fridge.

Roast Chicken with Tomato Kasundi

Roasted Lamb Loin with Lemon Grass

Lemon grass is stunning with both lamb and peaches! Make this dish when you have a supply of fresh lemon grass.

Serves 4

2 x 240 g lamb loin
2 tablespoons lemon grass oil (see below)
2 teaspoons soy sauce
black pepper, crushed
2 stalks lemon grass, sliced
4 bacon strips

Rub the lamb loin with lemon grass oil and season with soy sauce and crushed black pepper.

Lay the lemon grass around the lamb loin and wrap with bacon. Secure it with string. Pan-fry until the bacon is golden. Place in a 180°C oven and roast to the desired doneness – about 10 minutes for medium-rare – and allow to stand for 5 minutes.

Slice the lamb loin and serve. You can remove some of the lemon grass prior to serving but the flavour is just superb if the herb remains. Serve with Green Peppercorn Sauce (see page 112).

....

NOTE: To make lemon grass oil – steep some fresh, slightly crushed lemon grass in your favourite olive oil for 24 hours, then, just before using it, heat the oil (with the lemon grass) to just on boiling point to infuse the flavours.

Peach and Lemon Grass Compote

In Singapore, attending the Singapore Food Festival, I sampled both the scrumptious lamb with lemon grass and these amazing peaches with lemon grass. Singapore is a mecca for anyone who enjoys great food! **AW**

75 g lemon grass
3/4 cup sugar
750 ml water
4 peaches

Cut the lemon grass into pieces, combine with the sugar and water, and bring to the boil. Lower the heat and continue to cook until the flavour of the lemon grass has infused into the sugar syrup (about 30 minutes). Strain.

Peel the peaches and cut them into wedges. Add to the lemon grass flavoured syrup and cook over a low heat, until the peaches are soft and tender. Cool down to room temperature and then serve, with vanilla ice-cream.

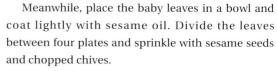

Pan-fried Asian-style Salmon with Crispy Orzo Cake

Orzo is a barley-shaped pasta, often mistaken for long-grain rice. It is a versatile ingredient in your pantry as it can make a delicious salad as well as an interesting accompaniment to stews and casseroles. It is available from specialty food stores.

Serves 4

4 x 90 g skinned and boned pieces salmon fillet

MARINADE:
$^1/_2$ **cup soy sauce**
2 tablespoons clear honey
1 teaspoon finely chopped ginger
1 tablespoon finely chopped coriander
salt and pepper

ORZO CAKE:
1 cup cooked orzo
1 egg
2 tablespoons flour
1 tablespoon finely chopped chives
$^1/_4$ **cup plain cooking oil**

GARNISH:
3 cups baby cress, mizuna or baby spinach
sesame oil
1$^1/_2$ tablespoons sesame seeds, toasted
1 tablespoon finely chopped chives

Mix the ingredients for the marinade well, season lightly with salt and pepper and place the salmon in the mixture to marinate for approximately 40 minutes, turning once or twice.

Mix the ingredients for the orzo cakes and rest for approximately 15 minutes. Heat the oven to 200°C. Heat a frypan with a good coating of cooking oil until just about smoking. Spoon the orzo mixture into four little cakes and fry both sides until crisp and golden brown. Transfer the cakes from the pan onto an oven tray and bake for about 10 minutes.

Meanwhile, place the baby leaves in a bowl and coat lightly with sesame oil. Divide the leaves between four plates and sprinkle with sesame seeds and chopped chives.

Heat the frypan until a good coating of oil is just smoking. Remove the salmon from the marinade and sear it, presentation side down, until crisp – approximately 2 minutes. Turn the salmon, lower the heat and cook for another 2 minutes.

Remove the orzo cakes from the oven. Put one on each plate, with a piece of salmon on top. Drizzle with sesame oil and serve.

....

NOTE: Mizuna is a Japanese green vegetable used as a garnish in Japanese cooking or in salads. For your garnish, if the gourmet greens listed are not available, use your favourite salad greens.

Always remember to heat your pan first, before adding the oil – you will use less oil with a heated pan.

Pan-fried Asian-style Salmon with Crispy Orzo Cake

Rib Eye of Beef with Roast Tomatoes, Parmesan Mash and Mustard Aioli

Stunning appearance and great flavours guaranteed!

Serves 4

1.5 kg rib eye beef
olive oil
salt and freshly ground black pepper
12 roast tomato halves
5 cups Parmesan Mash
1 cup Mustard Aioli

ROAST TOMATOES:
6 ripe medium tomatoes
1 teaspoon salt
1 teaspoon sugar
black pepper
olive oil

PARMESAN MASH:
5 cups hot mashed potatoes
1/2 cup cream
1/2 cup grated Parmesan
salt and freshly ground
  pepper

MUSTARD AIOLI (MAKES APPROX 1 CUP):
2 egg yolks
4 cloves garlic, finely chopped
1 tablespoon Dijon mustard
1/2 tablespoon lemon juice
1 cup olive oil
1 tablespoon warm water
salt and pepper

GARNISH:
1/3 cup olive oil
16 black Kalamata olives
1/2 cup baby rocket, watercress or spinach
3 tablespoons grated Parmesan

Roast Tomatoes: Preheat the oven to 230°C. Cut the tomatoes in half and place in a roasting tray. Sprinkle with salt and sugar. Grind over some black pepper and drizzle with olive oil. Roast for about 15 minutes at 230°C then turn the oven down to 100°C for about 2 hours.

Beef: Preheat the oven to 240°C. Rub the beef all over with olive oil and salt and pepper, then roast for 10 minutes. Turn the beef over and roast for another 5 minutes. Turn the oven down to 200°C, then roast for another 60 minutes. Wrap the beef loosely in foil and leave to rest for 15 minutes in a warm place, eg, a warming drawer or warm oven.

Parmesan Mash: Add the cream and Parmesan to hot mashed potatoes. Mix well and season with salt and pepper. Heating the cream gives better results.

Mustard Aioli: Put the egg yolks, garlic, mustard and lemon juice into a food processor. Turn the food processor on and add oil slowly in a thin stream until the mixture thickens. If it is too thick, add a little warm water. Season with salt and pepper.

ASSEMBLY:
Reheat the tomatoes at 160°C for 10 minutes. Warm the olive oil, olives and baby leaves in a saucepan or the microwave. Divide the Parmesan mash between four plates and place three tomato halves on top of each. Spoon the olive oil mixture onto the plates and dust with grated Parmesan. Slice the beef and place on top of the tomatoes. Drizzle with aioli and serve.

Rib Eye of Beef with Roast Tomatoes, Parmesan Mash and Mustard Aioli

Veal Brochette with Prosciutto and Sage

My good friend and fellow foodie Lauraine Jacobs devised this delicious veal and prosciutto dish. The sage adds a great flavour sensation. **KP**

peel of 1 lemon, removed
    with a vegetable peeler
2 tablespoons fresh lemon
    juice
$1/4$ cup olive oil
1 medium clove garlic,
    peeled and crushed
1 kg veal fillet cut into
    5 cm cubes
9 pieces thinly sliced
    prosciutto, cut in half
18 fresh sage leaves
6 skewers
salt and black pepper

Make a marinade, combining the lemon peel, lemon juice, olive oil and garlic. Place the cubes of veal in this and cover well. Marinate overnight.

Take out the veal cubes, reserving the marinade, and place each cube on a slice of prosciutto, with a sage leaf. Wrap up and place three cubes on each skewer.

Preheat the grill. Sprinkle the brochettes with salt and pepper, and brush with some of the marinade. Grill about 10 cm from the heat until lightly browned. Turn, brush with marinade and grill for a further 5 minutes. The centre should be lightly pink.

Garnish with lemon slices or preserved lemons and fresh sage, and serve with Lemon Sage Butter.

Lemon Sage Butter

150 g softened butter
grated peel of 1 medium lemon
2 tablespoons fresh lemon juice
2 tablespoons sage leaves

Process all the ingredients in a food processor until smooth. Serve slightly chilled.

'Each of us eats about one thousand meals each year. It is my belief that we should try and make as many of these meals as we can truly memorable.'

Robert Carrier

**Veal Brochette with
Prosciutto and Sage**

Layered Meringue Cake

Kathy loves to prepare the simple classics and I always joke with her that this Layered Meringue Cake is not a dessert – it's a statement. Crunchy, sweet meringue mixed with whipped cream and topped with tart, full-flavoured fruit coulis. Heaven was never more accessible.   **AW**

Serves 12

6 egg whites (6 fl oz or
**   175 ml)**
340 g caster sugar
600 ml cream
icing sugar

Whisk egg whites until stiff, add 6 teaspoons of the measured sugar and whisk for 20 seconds. Cut and fold in the remaining sugar. Do not over-fold as it becomes too soft.

Line two baking trays with baking paper. Using a piping bag with a 2.5 cm eclair nozzle, pipe the meringue into two circles on the baking paper, or spoon the meringue into two even rounds. Bake at 120–130°C for 2 hours until a light beige colour or the rounds peel off the paper easily. Turn the oven off and leave to cool.

Fill the meringue with cream at least 2 hours before serving, to allow for easy cutting. Whip the cream until stiff and use it to sandwich the two flat sides of the meringue together. Dust with icing sugar.

....

NOTE: I always measure out my egg whites as I keep them in a jar in the refrigerator or freeze them.   **KP**

Fruit Coulis

You can use any berry fruit for a fruit coulis. With the Layered Meringue Cake we used strawberries, but for the Apricot Bread and Butter Pudding we recommend raspberries. Please note, always strain your raspberry coulis to remove any seeds.

2 chips strawberries
icing sugar to taste

Hull the strawberries and purée in a food processor. Add icing sugar to bring out the flavour.

Fruit Ice-cream

Former Cordon Bleu teacher and fellow foodie, Anna Hughes, gave me this recipe years ago. It's still a big favourite and deliciously easy.   **KP**

4 egg whites (4 fl oz or ¹/₂ cup)
1 cup caster sugar
300 ml fruit purée
300 ml cream, half whipped

Whisk the egg whites, adding the sugar slowly until the mixture is very stiff. Fold the fruit purée and cream together, then fold through the egg white mix.

I put this in a glass loaf dish lined with plastic wrap or baking paper. Cover well and freeze overnight. Eat within one week.

....

NOTE: If using strawberry purée, cut back the sugar to 170 g. If using plums, remove the stones but leave the skin on. If using raspberries, sieve to remove seeds.

Anna's Boozy Stuffed Prunes

My sister, Anna, makes these. They are great with coffee, any time! **KP**

18 prunes
300 ml dessert wine
100 g mascarpone
4 tablespoons blanched
   almonds, toasted and
   chopped
grated rind of 1 orange
100 g chocolate
icing sugar

Soak the prunes overnight in wine. Drain the prunes and place on baking paper. Mix together the mascarpone, almonds and orange rind. With a teaspoon or a piping bag with a plain nozzle place the mascarpone mixture on top of the prunes. Melt the chocolate (in the microwave or over hot water) and drizzle over the stuffed prunes. Allow to set then sprinkle with icing sugar.

NOTE: You can also make this recipe with figs instead of prunes.

Apricot Bread and Butter Pudding

Serves 4

50 g soft butter
6 slices white bread
$1/2$ tablespoon cinnamon
12 tinned or preserved apricot quarters
3 tablespoons sultanas
1 cup milk
$4^1/2$ tablespoons sugar
2 eggs
$1/2$ tablespoon vanilla essence

Lightly butter four soufflé dishes. Butter the slices of bread and cut off the crusts. Cut each slice into four triangles. Line each dish with four triangles of bread, slightly overlapping. Lightly dust with cinnamon, then put two apricot quarters and approximately 5 sultanas in each dish. Place two more triangles of bread in the centre over the sultanas and apricots, then put another piece of apricot in each dish. Sprinkle with the remaining sultanas and lightly dust with cinnamon.

Warm the milk. Whisk the sugar, eggs and vanilla together, then pour the warm milk over the mixture and mix well. Pour the yolk mixture evenly between the four dishes. Place the dishes in a roasting tray half-filled with water. Carefully place in an oven that has been preheated to 180°C and cook for 25–30 minutes. When cooked, let rest for 5 minutes, then either turn out or serve in the dishes. Dust with icing sugar before serving.

NOTE: Serve with vanilla ice-cream, raspberry coulis, whipped cream or thin custard.

'I am a pudding man. Nothing depresses
me more than a meal which doesn't
finish with one. "Just coffee for me, thanks"
is not a phrase in my book.
However boring the occasion, I perk up when
they wheel in the sweet trolley.'

Robert Morley

**Apricot Bread and
Butter Pudding**

Barbecues

Mention the word 'barbecue' and people's
eyes light up. There is a magic about cooking
outdoors – the aroma of grilling food, the sizzle
and the smoke. So chill those drinks, marinate
some food and fire up the barbecue ...
roll on summer!

Fresh New Zealand Scallops with a Gazpacho Sauce

Allow 6–8 scallops per person

SAUCE:

3 egg yolks
1/4 teaspoon Dijon mustard
1 cup olive oil
salt and pepper
3 cloves garlic, crushed
1/4–1/2 small cucumber, puréed (with skin) for juice
1/2 cup thick tomato juice or 1 tablespoon tomato paste
fresh dill or basil

Make a mayonnaise by placing the egg yolks and mustard in the bowl of a food processor. Process for a few minutes until well blended, then slowly drizzle in the oil. This should become very thick. Add the salt and pepper, garlic, cucumber juice and tomato juice to the mayonnaise until it is a sauce with a good pouring consistency. Place in a small saucepan. Carefully warm the sauce but do not boil as it will curdle.

Barbecue or quickly pan-fry the scallops in a little hot oil until they change colour. This will only take a few seconds.

Pour the sauce onto each plate. Arrange the scallops and sprinkle with fresh dill or small pieces of basil.

Basic Seafood Marinade

This is a multi-use marinade, ideal for seafood.

1 tablespoon minced garlic
1 tablespoon minced fresh ginger
1/3 cup fresh lemon juice
2 cups canola or grapeseed oil
1 bay leaf, crumbled
sea salt and freshly ground black pepper

Combine the garlic, ginger and lemon juice together in a non-reactive bowl. Whisk in the oil a little at a time. Add the bay leaf and salt and pepper.

NOTE: Do not over-marinate seafood – best to consider the thickness of your fish fillets, for example, and vary your marinating time accordingly. Allow 30–60 minutes for fish according to the thickness of the fillets.

Basic Chicken Marinade

1 kg chicken pieces
1/3 cup hoisin sauce
1/3 cup orange juice
1 spring onion, finely chopped
1 tablespoon white vinegar
1 tablespoon honey
1 teaspoon sesame oil
3 cloves garlic, minced

Just put the ingredients into a resealable plastic bag and place it in the fridge for at least 1–2 hours. When you are ready, preheat the grill, remove the meat from the marinade and cook, turning each piece only once.

NOTE: This marinade works just as well with red meat as it does with chicken.

Hot Pineapple Dish

This dish is a family tradition with the barbecued ham on the bone at Christmas in our house. The recipe was collected at a pot-luck supper in Dover, Delaware, in the United States, when I was an AFS high school student. If you are invited to a barbecue, this is the ideal contribution. It is best eaten warm and can be reheated the next day.　**AW**

Serves 6 as an accompaniment

125 g butter
5 slices of toast bread
432 g can crushed pineapple
$^1/_2$ cup sugar
2 tablespoons flour
pinch of salt
2 eggs

Melt the butter in a large bowl and reserve. Remove the crusts from the bread and cut into cubes about 2.5 cm square. Add the bread cubes to the melted butter, turn gently and coat with butter.

Place the crushed pineapple, sugar, flour and salt in another bowl. Beat the eggs lightly and add to the pineapple mixture. Place the pineapple mix in a buttered 18–20 cm ovenproof gratin dish. Spread the buttered bread cubes on top of the mix and bake at 180°C for 30–40 minutes.

....

NOTE: This is also delicious with barbecued pork sausages and grilled chicken. It may sound like a dessert, but it is delicious with savoury food.

Michael's Grilled Chicken

Several years ago, top Auckland chef Michael James served a group of food writers this tasty chicken dish at a chicken lunch. The combination of Asian flavours with deliciously moist chicken had us begging for more.

Serves 4

8 chicken thighs or breasts, skinned and boned

MARINADE:
$^1/_2$ cup Thai sweet chilli sauce
$^1/_4$ cup coconut milk

2 tablespoons lime juice
1–2 tablespoons coriander, finely chopped
2 tablespoons chopped roasted peanuts
2 teaspoons sweet soy sauce

Mix all the ingredients together, including the chicken, and leave for 4–5 hours before barbecuing. Alternatively, they can be grilled for 10 minutes in the oven.

Beef with Rocket

Serves 8

1.5 kg (approx) eye fillet of beef
good quality olive oil or truffle oil
freshly ground black pepper
1 cup rocket
salt and pepper

Lightly oil the eye fillet. Sprinkle with freshly ground black pepper. Cook for 20 minutes on the barbecue, turning to cook all sides. Alternatively, place the fillet on a baking tray, sprinkle with freshly ground black pepper and a dash of oil and cook in your oven for 20 minutes at 210°C for medium/rare on fan bake.

Leave to rest for 10 minutes, covered loosely with foil, then slice. Sprinkle with rocket then with oil and serve.

Chargrilled Vegetables with Yoghurt Dressing

Everyone loves chargrilled vegetables – just the sight of brilliantly coloured capsicums and wedges of zucchini and eggplant makes everyone happy.

Serves 6–8

1 eggplant
1 large red onion
6 small to medium zucchini
3 red or yellow capsicums
6 vine-ripened tomatoes
olive oil

YOGHURT DRESSING:
1 cup sour cream
1 cup unsweetened yoghurt
salt, black pepper and sugar to taste
6 tablespoons fresh basil, shredded or pulled
    into pieces
juice of 1 lemon

Slice the eggplant into rounds 1 cm thick. Lightly brush with olive oil and barbecue on a hot grill. Cut the onion in half and then cut into thin slices. Cook with a little olive oil on the hot plate. Cut the zucchini in half lengthwise and grill on a hot grill. Cut the capsicums in half, deseed and cut again. Grill on a hot grill. Cut the tomatoes into halves or quarters. There is no need to cook them.

Place all the vegetables on a large serving platter. Pour over some of the dressing and serve the rest separately.

Dressing: Combine all the ingredients, adding the lemon juice last.

....

NOTE: Instead of the dressing you can sprinkle over a little good red wine vinegar.

Skewered Prawns with Pawpaw Salsa

Simple, sensational flavours – perfect for a special cook-out!

PAWPAW SALSA:

1 pawpaw

2 spring onions, finely sliced

1 tablespoon finely shredded mint or basil

2–3 tablespoons sweet chilli sauce

raw king prawns – leave shell, head and
   tail on

metal skewers

Peel and dice pawpaw into even-sized cubes and place in a bowl. Add the spring onions, mint or basil, and chilli sauce. Cover and allow the flavours to develop for approximately 1 hour before serving.

Thread 3–4 king prawns onto each skewer. Barbecue on a hot grill until the prawns turn pink. Do not overcook as they will be rubbery. Serve with the pawpaw salsa, plenty of napkins and a finger bowl each.

....

NOTE: You can use wooden skewers instead of metal ones, but if you do, don't forget to soak them overnight before use on the barbecue, so they won't catch fire!

Mustard-Soy Marinade

This is a favourite in-a-hurry marinade – it's fast, simple and tasty!

$1/3$ cup grainy mustard

$1/4$ cup rice wine vinegar

$1/2$ cup light soy sauce

$1/2$–1 teaspoon Tabasco

1 tablespoon dark brown sugar

Combine the ingredients in a bowl and place in a resealable plastic bag with one of the following:

SALMON – marinate for 1 hour

CHICKEN BREASTS – marinate for 2–4 hours

RIBS – marinate overnight

LEG OF LAMB – marinate overnight.

'You want to spread
a little happiness, *non*?'

Paul Bocuse

Skewered Prawns
with Pawpaw Salsa

Chickpea Purée

Watch this purée disappear and all your guests ask for the recipe – it's so popular!

2 cups chickpeas, soaked
  overnight in plenty of
  cold water
salt
lemon juice
3 cloves garlic, crushed
olive oil

Drain and rinse the chickpeas. Place in a saucepan, cover with fresh water and cook until tender (30–45 minutes). Add salt just before the end of cooking. Drain.

Place the chickpeas in a food processor with plenty of lemon juice and the garlic. Drizzle in enough olive oil to give you a soft purée. Taste and season.

Serve with hot toast, Lebanese crisps or Sourdough Croutes.

....

NOTE: When soaking chickpeas make sure they are covered by about 10 cm of cold water.

Sourdough Croutes

Sourdough bread makes the best croutes as they cook evenly and stay crunchy.

Slice a sourdough baguette into thin rounds (approximately 5 mm). Brush both sides with olive oil and place on a baking tray. Bake at 190°C until they turn golden to mid-brown. Cool on a wire rack. Store in an airtight container.

Croutes will keep for one week.

Tuna with Green Olive and Anchovy Relish

lemon peel from 1 lemon, peeled with a
  vegetable peeler
2 tablespoons olive oil
2 cloves garlic, crushed
salt and pepper
500 g fresh tuna, cut into bite-size chunks

GREEN OLIVE AND ANCHOVY RELISH:
$^1/_2$ cup green olives stuffed with anchovies,
  chopped
$^1/_2$ cup chopped Italian parsley
1 tablespoon chardonnay vinegar or other
  white wine vinegar
1 clove garlic, crushed
$^1/_4$ cup extra virgin olive oil
oil for cooking

Combine the lemon peel, olive oil, garlic and salt and pepper in a bowl. Marinate the tuna in this for 2 hours.

Mix the ingredients for the relish well.

Smear a little oil on the barbecue or in a frypan. In batches, sauté the marinated chunks of tuna until just browned.

Serve the cooked tuna in china spoons (available from Asian stores), topped with relish, as a canapé before lunch or dinner.

....

NOTE: Kingfish or any other dense white fish also works well.

Seafood Salad with Ginger-Lime Dressing

A salad of prawns and crabmeat gets a little tropical treatment with a refreshing ginger-lime dressing. This creamy topping also works well with chargrilled chicken.

Serves 4–6

GINGER-LIME DRESSING:

3/4 cup mayonnaise

1/2 cup fresh parsley leaves

4 teaspoons fresh lime juice

1 1/2 teaspoons grated lime zest

1 1/2 teaspoons grated fresh ginger

3/4 cup plain low-fat yoghurt

SEAFOOD SALAD:

500 g crabmeat

2 teaspoons lime juice

750 g cooked prawns, shelled and deveined

assorted salad greens

1/2 melon, peeled and sliced

2 mangoes, peeled and sliced

1 cucumber, thinly sliced

First, make the dressing. Combine the mayonnaise, parsley, lime juice, zest and ginger in a blender or food processor and blend until smooth. Transfer to a bowl and stir in the yoghurt. This can be made ahead of time.

Toss the crabmeat with the lime juice and 1/2 cup of the dressing. Arrange the rest of the salad ingredients on a large platter and drizzle some more of the dressing over the top before serving.

....

NOTE: Any remaining dressing can be placed in a side dish for dunking the prawns into as you enjoy your salad.

Roasted Red Capsicum Relish

Roasted Red Capsicum Relish is a versatile accompaniment to your chargrilled vegetables and meats. You can start your barbecue by serving this relish with bread or you can mix half cup relish with half cup yoghurt to make a dipping sauce for seafood.

1/2 cup olive oil

1 cup chopped onions

750 g red capsicums, skinned and cut into thin strips

1 cup red wine vinegar

750 g plum tomatoes, canned or fresh

1 cup sugar

1 cup golden raisins or sultanas

2 large cloves garlic, crushed

2 teaspoons fresh ginger, peeled and grated

1/2 teaspoon salt

1/2 teaspoon ground allspice

2 red chillies, finely chopped

Put the oil and onions into a large, heavy-based saucepan. Cook over a low heat until the onions are translucent. Add the capsicum strips and vinegar. Boil until the vinegar is reduced by half.

Purée and sieve the tomatoes and then measure two cups. Add to the capsicum and vinegar mixture along with the sugar, raisins, garlic, ginger, salt, allspice and chillies. Cover partially with a lid and cook over a low heat until thick, stirring occasionally.

Let the relish cool, then store in clean jars in the refrigerator.

....

NOTE: If using fresh tomatoes you will need to skin them first by plunging them into boiling water for 6–8 seconds and then into cold water.

Falafel Fritters

I really enjoy eating chickpeas and this recipe is a good one. It was perfected by Jo Cooper, who worked in catering with me some years ago. **KP**

Serves 6

2 cups chickpeas, soaked overnight in plenty
   of cold water
1 teaspoon salt
3 cloves garlic, crushed
3 stalks celery, lightly peeled to remove stringy
   parts, then chopped
3 spring onions, chopped
1/2 cup chopped parsley
1 teaspoon ground cumin
1 teaspoon turmeric
1/4 teaspoon cayenne
   pepper
1 egg, lightly beaten
flour to coat

Drain and rinse the chickpeas. Place in a large saucepan, cover well with cold water and boil until soft (about 30–40 minutes). Just before they are completely soft, add the salt. Drain. Mash the chickpeas well and combine with the other ingredients. Taste for seasoning. Chill well.

With floured hands, make 5 cm fritters. Dust each fritter lightly with flour and cook on a lightly oiled hot plate on your barbecue. Alternatively, cook in a frypan. Serve with a spicy fruit chutney or unsweetened yoghurt and chopped fresh mint.

Moroccan Paste

This paste is delicious with your lamb chops or smear it over lamb kebabs before cooking. This recipe will be enough for about 1 kg of cubed lamb.

Serves 4–6

3 tablespoons lime juice
1/4 cup olive oil
1/4 cup finely chopped fresh parsley
1 small onion, finely chopped
3 cloves garlic, minced
1 tablespoon sea salt
1 tablespoon freshly ground pepper
   1 tablespoon paprika
   1 tablespoon ground
      cumin
   1 tablespoon ground
      coriander seeds

Make the marinade by combining all the ingredients in a resealable bag then place the meat inside. Allow 2–24 hours for marinating.

....

NOTE: Some flavour enthusiasts say they marinate the meat for even longer – experiment and enjoy the results.

'I love Morocco ...
it has one of the truly great cuisines in the world –
not in its restaurants and snack bars,
but in its private homes.'

Robert Carrier

Moroccan Paste on Lamb Racks

Grilled Lemon-Oregano Chicken Salad

Serves 4–6

$1/2$ teaspoon grated lemon peel

2 tablespoons fresh lemon juice

1 tablespoon olive oil

1 tablespoon chopped fresh oregano

2–4 cloves garlic, minced

$1/2$ teaspoon salt

4 boneless, skinless chicken breast halves

6 cups torn lettuce leaves

1 punnet cherry tomatoes

DRESSING:

$1/3$ cup mayonnaise

$1/3$ cup buttermilk

$3/4$ teaspoon grated lemon peel

1 teaspoon fresh lemon juice

$1/2$ teaspoon minced garlic

$1/4$ teaspoon salt

Combine lemon peel, lemon juice, oil, oregano, garlic and salt in a resealable plastic bag. Add chicken and seal the bag, turn to coat and refrigerate for 2 hours.

Make the dressing by whisking together the mayonnaise, buttermilk, lemon peel, lemon juice, garlic and salt in a bowl. Cover and refrigerate.

Meanwhile, heat the grill and grill the chicken – allowing 5 minutes per side, turning only once. Slice, after a few minutes resting.

To serve, arrange the lettuce, tomatoes and chicken on four plates and drizzle the dressing over the top.

....

NOTE: Buttermilk is a great bonus to have in the fridge. Commercial buttermilk lasts forever and makes a great addition to scones, pancakes and even dressings! If you cannot find buttermilk at your local supermarket then just substitute with plain, non-fat yoghurt.

Fresh Summer Fruit Cake

This is an ideal dessert to bring to a barbecue. The topping varies according to the season. Early summer will see berries and late summer, slices of stone fruits. Either way it is so easy, yet looks very elegant. Best eaten fresh, it is almost like a tart.

$1^1/4$ cups flour

$3/4$ cup sugar

120 g butter, melted

2 eggs

approx 4 cups sliced seasonal fruit

2 tablespoons sugar

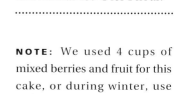

Blend the flour and sugar together. Add the melted butter and eggs. Pour the mixture into a greased, loose-bottomed 24 cm cake tin.

Slice the seasonal fruit, leaving the skin on any stone fruits (plums, apricots, nectarines, peaches). Place the fruit on top of the cake, piling it up and pressing down a little. Sprinkle with the sugar and bake at 180°C for 1 hour.

....

NOTE: We used 4 cups of mixed berries and fruit for this cake, or during winter, use drained, canned fruits.

Fresh Summer Fruit Cake

Barbecued Fresh Fruits

With summer arriving, so do the beautiful stone fruits. Use any stone fruits, eg, free-stone peaches, nectarines or apricots.

stone fruit
grated lime rind
lime juice
brown sugar

Wash and dry the fruit. Cut in half and remove the stones. Place the fruit cut-side down on a hot grill. Cook until the fruit is hot. Allow 2–3 minutes for ripe fruits. Harder fruits will need a little longer. You may need to turn larger pieces of fruit over.

Serve hot off the grill with grated lime rind and juice. Pass the brown sugar.

....

NOTE: Try serving with yoghurt or softened ice-cream with Lemon Curd (see page 38) stirred through.

Grilled golden queen peaches are delicious served with almond biscuits (amaretto). As they are cling-stone, you will need to cut peaches either side of the stone for better results.

Another suggestion is to serve your grilled fruits with fresh raspberry sauce – just purée 2 cups of raspberries. Rub through a nylon or stainless steel sieve to remove seeds. Whisk in icing sugar to sweeten and bring out the flavour of the raspberries.

Citron Pressé

SUGAR SYRUP:
1 cup sugar
1 cup boiling water

lemon juice
sparkling mineral water

Place the sugar and water in a heavy-based saucepan. Heat until the sugar is dissolved and then boil quickly until a thick syrup is formed. Do not allow the syrup to colour or you will end up with caramel. Cool and pour into shot glasses.

Fill a long glass for each person with plenty of ice and some lemon juice, then allow them to add sugar syrup from a shot glass and sparkling mineral water to taste.

Fireside Suppers

Contentment comes easily by the glow and warmth of an open fire. It is a chance to ease back and serve delicious comfort food. This is the time for soups, stews, grandma's puddings and anything easily eaten out of a sturdy bowl. Some friends and family you would invite for lunch or dinner, but it is the particularly close friend (who thinks you look glamorous in your scruffy sweats) whom you invite to supper!

Cajun Vegetable Stew

My fellow foodie and friend, Grahame Dawson, shared this recipe with me. Don't let the number of ingredients put you off – this is divine. **KP**

Serves 8–10

2 tablespoons oil

2 cups onions, chopped into 2.5 cm dice

2 tablespoons chopped garlic

2 tablespoons ground coriander

$1/2$ teaspoon nutmeg

$1/2$ teaspoon allspice

1 teaspoon cumin

2 cups pumpkin, peeled and chopped into 1.5 cm dice

1 cup kumara, peeled and chopped into 1.5 cm dice

1 red capsicum, seeded and chopped

2–4 bird's eye chillies, chopped

1 sliced green banana

400 g whole peeled tomatoes, roughly chopped

400 ml coconut cream

425 g can whole kernel corn, drained

1 teaspoon thyme

2 teaspoons oregano

$1/2$ cup orange juice

$1/4$ teaspoon salt

pinch pepper or to taste

1 tablespoon finely chopped coriander

Heat the oil and cook the onion until soft but not coloured. Add the garlic, ground coriander, nutmeg, allspice and cumin and cook for 30 seconds. Add the pumpkin, kumara, capsicum and chillies. When the vegetables have a coating of the spices, add the sliced banana, tomatoes, coconut cream, corn, thyme, oregano and orange juice, and season with salt and pepper.

Cover and simmer on a very low heat for 60 minutes or until tender. The vegetables should still be whole rather than mushy. Add the chopped coriander at the end, prior to serving.

Brown Pinenut Bread

This is a gutsy, rustic loaf with a very crusty top. Serve with Cajun Vegetable Stew for a tasty fireside supper.

Makes 2 loaves

$1^1/4$ cups plain flour

1 teaspoon salt

2 teaspoons baking powder

$1^1/2$ teaspoons baking soda

4 cups wholemeal flour

$1^1/4$ cups unprocessed bran

2 cups (250 g) pinenuts

2 cups (500 ml) plain unsweetened yoghurt

1 cup warm water

Sift the plain flour, salt, baking powder and baking soda into a mixing bowl. Add the wholemeal flour, bran and pinenuts. Stir in the yoghurt and the warm water to achieve a soft dough.

Divide between two well-greased large loaf tins and bake at 190°C for 30–40 minutes. Place a skewer in the middle of each loaf. If it comes out clean the bread is cooked. Cool in the tin for 5 minutes, then turn out onto a rack.

....

NOTE: This bread freezes well.

Ham Puffs

Makes about 45 puffs

250 g or 1 cup cream cheese, softened
1 egg yolk
1 teaspoon baking powder
dash of salt
10–12 thin slices white sandwich bread
mayonnaise
thin slices of ham
paprika

Combine the cream cheese with the egg yolk, baking powder and salt. Mix until blended and smooth.

Cut about four small rounds from each slice of bread, using a scone cutter. Spread each round lightly with mayonnaise. Cover each with a slice of ham. Spoon the cheese mixture on the ham, and sprinkle with paprika. This much can be done ahead of time and frozen if you wish. To serve, place in a 190°C oven for 12–15 minutes, or until puffed and browned. Serve immediately.

Cauliflower Soup

We added crumbled blue cheese to this soup in each serving bowl. It was presented to our fireside guests with a flourish!

Serves 4

1 onion, diced
3 rashers bacon, rind removed
3 cloves garlic, minced
1 tablespoon butter
1 cauliflower, broken into florets
5 cups chicken stock
3–4 tablespoons butter

2–3 tablespoons flour
1 cup milk
salt and freshly ground
    black pepper

GARNISH:
blue cheese, crumbled
cream
fresh coriander

Cook the onion, bacon and garlic in the first measure of butter. When the onion is soft and translucent, add the cauliflower and gently toss to cover the florets in some of the onion mixture. Add the chicken stock and gently simmer until the vegetables are soft.

Meanwhile prepare a simple roux by melting the butter, adding the flour and cooking for 1–2 minutes carefully. Season with salt and pepper and add milk. Stir until the mixture thickens, taking care to ensure it does not catch.

Process or blend the cauliflower in the chicken stock. Add the thickened roux and check the seasoning. Reheat gently. Serve with crumbled blue cheese or a little swirl of cream. Top with coriander.

'A home is a place where a pot of fresh soup simmers gently on the hob, filling the kitchen with soft aromas ... and filling your heart, and later your tummy, with joy.'

Keith Floyd

Cauliflower Soup

Risotto with Pumpkin

We have specified arborio rice for this risotto. It is readily available in supermarkets.

Serves 6

2 cups diced butternut
   pumpkin
2 tablespoons olive oil
2 tablespoons butter
1 small onion, chopped
1 cup arborio rice
4–4$^1/_2$ cups boiling water
$^1/_4$ cup good quality white
   wine
salt and black pepper
$^1/_2$ cup grated Parmesan

Peel and seed the pumpkin. Cut into small cubes.

Place 2 tablespoons of oil and 1 tablespoon of butter in a large heavy-based pan. Cook the onion until soft but not coloured. Add the rice and stir until well coated with oil. Add the pumpkin, one cup of the measured water and the wine. Season with salt and pepper. Once the water has been absorbed, add another cup and continue adding water in this way until the rice is cooked – about 30 minutes. Remove from the heat and add the remaining tablespoon of butter and the Parmesan.

....

NOTE: Serve with extra Parmesan, crusty bread and a mixed green salad. Pass the salt and pepper.

Mediterranean Roast Lamb

This Mediterranean-inspired lamb is delicious served with oven-roasted vegetables with fresh rosemary, minted peas and a roasted red capsicum salad.

Serves 4–6

1.8 kg leg of lamb
3 cloves garlic, peeled and cut in half
   lengthways
1 small lemon, rind and juice
fresh rosemary
salt and pepper
$^3/_4$ cup finely chopped black Kalamata olives
2–3 tablespoons fresh breadcrumbs
1 egg
5 anchovy fillets, rolled in circles and cut
   in half

Preheat the oven to 220°C. Make approximately 4–6 slits in the surface of the lamb. Slide slices of garlic and lemon peel and rosemary sprigs into the slits. Season with salt and pepper. Cook for 20 minutes at 220°C. Turn the oven down to 190°C and cook for 40 minutes.

Make a paste by combining the olives, breadcrumbs and the egg.

Remove the lamb from the oven. Remove the rosemary and the lemon peel. Cool slightly, then coat the surface of the lamb with the olive paste, dot with the anchovy fillets and bake for another 20–25 minutes. Cover the lamb in tin foil and let it rest for 15 minutes before serving.

Baked Ricotta

This is great for an antipasti platter. Serve with a fresh tomato salsa or relish.

Serves 6

3 tablespoons extra virgin olive oil
2 tablespoons dry breadcrumbs
400 g ricotta
1 egg, lightly beaten
4 tablespoons grated Parmesan
$^1/_2$–1 teaspoon fresh thyme, chopped, or fresh
    rosemary, chopped
salt and freshly ground black pepper

Oil a 12 cm soufflé dish with 1$^1/_2$ tablespoons of the olive oil. Coat the inside of the dish with breadcrumbs. Tap out the excess.

If the ricotta is wet, drain it in a cheese-cloth. Combine the ricotta, egg and Parmesan. Season to taste with herbs and salt and pepper. Pour the mixture into the prepared dish. Drizzle the remaining oil evenly over the top. Bake at 190°C for 40 minutes or until it is golden and firm on top.

Olive Bread

This bread is lovely served with a fresh, chunky tomato soup and a wedge of good Parmesan.

1 cup milk
1 tablespoon sugar
3 teaspoons dried yeast
6 egg yolks
4 cups flour
1 teaspoon salt
150 g butter, softened
1 cup black olives, chopped
1 tablespoon chopped rosemary or thyme

Heat the milk and sugar until lukewarm. Sprinkle the yeast over the milk and allow to froth (approximately 5 minutes). Beat the egg yolks lightly and add to the yeast mixture.

Place the flour and salt in a large bowl. Pour in the yeast mixture and mix to a dough. After working well (I use an electric mixer with a dough hook or a food processor), add butter and continue to work until smooth and glossy. Cover the bowl with plastic wrap and leave to rise until the mixture has doubled in size.

Push the dough down and add the olives and herbs. Form into the desired shape or place in a well-greased loaf tin or savarin tin. Cover and leave to rise again (generally to the top of the tin).

Bake at 190°C for about 30 minutes. Test with a skewer in the centre of the loaf or turn out of the tin and tap the base of the bread – it should sound hollow.

'The whole Mediterranean ...
all of it seems to rise in the sour, pungent smell
of these black olives between the teeth.
A taste older than meat, older than wine.
A taste as old as cold water.'

Lawrence Durrell

Eggplant Fritters

The wine in these fritters improves the flavour, and the sparkling mineral water lightens the batter.

Serves 4

1 egg

$1/4$ cup dry white wine

$1/2$ cup sparkling mineral
    water

1 cup flour

1 clove garlic, crushed

salt and pepper

1 tablespoon fresh
    coriander, chopped

1 eggplant

sea salt

Mix all the above ingredients, except the eggplant and the sea salt, together in a food processor or bowl and whisk into a batter.

Cut the eggplant in half lengthwise and sprinkle with half a teaspoon of salt. Leave for half an hour, then wipe dry with a paper towel. Slice into 1 cm slices. Dip the eggplant into the batter and fry in hot oil until golden brown, turning once. Drain on paper towels, sprinkle with sea salt and serve immediately.

Tomato and Olive Frittata

This is great to make when the fridge and pantry are running low and you want a quick and easy supper. Easy to digest, this would make an ideal after-theatre supper treat. Just make the tomato sauce earlier in the day and whip up the eggs as you light the fire.

Serves 4

2–3 tablespoons oil

4 cloves garlic, minced

1 large onion, diced

2 tomatoes, diced and core removed

1 tablespoon tomato paste

1 tablespoon freshly chopped oregano

salt and pepper

$1/2$ teaspoon sugar

6 eggs

additional olive oil

$1/2$ cup Parmesan

10–12 olives, pitted

Heat the oil in a heavy-bottomed frypan and add the garlic and onion. When the onion is translucent and soft, add the tomatoes and tomato paste. Add the oregano, seasoning and sugar. Cook on low for 20–30 minutes. It will reduce down, so stir from time to time. Do not rush this stage as the flavours need slow cooking to develop. Let the tomato mixture cool a little.

Gently beat the eggs (for a great result the secret is to barely beat them). Add 3 generous tablespoons of the tomato sauce to the eggs. Add additional oil to the frypan and when hot add the egg mixture. Cook slowly, tipping the pan to ensure even cooking. When the eggs are just set, scatter the cheese and olives over the top and place under the grill for a few minutes until the top sets. Do not overcook the frittata. Err on the side of under-cooking the eggs.

....

NOTE: You will make extra tomato sauce in this recipe – cover and keep in the fridge for another frittata or perhaps eat it with cold meats or grilled fish.

Thai Mussel Stir Fry

Don't let the number of ingredients put you off this recipe. It is a great treatment of inexpensive mussels. You can also add squid to this recipe for a delicious result.

Serves 6

1 kg mussels
400 ml white wine
1 tablespoon chopped root ginger
2 cloves garlic
1 small onion, sliced
2 chillies, finely chopped
1 large capsicum, chopped
2 Kaffir lime leaves
2 tablespoons fish sauce
400 ml coconut cream
2 limes, freshly squeezed
200 g or 1 cup broccoli, blanched
200 g or 1 cup snowpeas, blanched
500 g fresh laksa noodles or 200 g dried
    rice vermicelli
2 tablespoons chopped fresh coriander

Steam the mussels lightly in the wine, then shell, reserving the juice.

Make sure the wok is very hot, then sauté the ginger, garlic, onion, chillies, capsicum and lime leaves.

Now put in the mussels for a few seconds until they are coated in the mixture. Remove the mussels and reserve. Now put the fish sauce, coconut cream, lime juice and the reserved mussel juice into the wok and reduce for 5 minutes on a high heat. Add the coated mussels, followed by the blanched broccoli, snowpeas and noodles. Garnish with chopped coriander.

....

NOTE: Dried Kaffir lime leaves are available from Asian supply stores and can be used after pre-soaking. Kaffir lime trees are becoming available from the markets and are a good investment for your kitchen garden. Chop the leaves up and they will impart a delicate citrus fragrance and flavour.

To prepare the laksa noodles (available from Asian supply stores) just pour hot water through them. If using rice vermicelli, soak in very hot water for 10 minutes, then drain.

Lemon Chicken

You can prepare half this recipe if desired.

Serves 6–8

2 whole chickens (1.2–1.5 kg each), quartered
2$\frac{1}{2}$ cups fresh lemon juice (about 10 lemons)
1 cup flour
1 tablespoon paprika
salt and freshly ground black pepper to taste
1 cup chicken stock
2$\frac{1}{2}$ tablespoons brown sugar
1 lemon, thinly sliced
1 tablespoon herbs de Provence

One day before serving, place the chicken pieces in a shallow dish. Pour the lemon juice over the chicken and marinate in the refrigerator overnight, turning the pieces occasionally.

Preheat the oven to 190°C. Remove the chicken from the lemon juice, reserving the juice. Combine the flour, paprika and salt and pepper. Dredge the chicken with the seasoned flour and place skin side up in a shallow baking pan. Bake for 40 minutes.

While the chicken is baking, whisk the reserved lemon juice, the stock, brown sugar and lemon slices together. Pour the lemon mixture over the chicken and sprinkle with herbs de Provence. Bake 20–25 minutes more, basting occasionally with the pan juices.

You can serve this dish hot, at room temperature, or serve it cold.

Thai Mussel Stir Fry

Spiced Fruit Compote

Serves 12

2 lapsang souchong tea bags
3 cups boiling water
3 pitted prunes per person
3 dried apricots or pears, peaches, nectarines
   or figs per person

1 x 750 ml bottle red wine, good quality
2¹/₄ cups caster sugar
1 vanilla pod, split in half
1 bay leaf
1 cinnamon stick
12 peppercorns
12 star anise
rind of 1 lemon or orange
   or lime

6 fresh pears
lemon juice

Make a weak tea in a saucepan using the lapsang tea bags and the boiling water. Add the dried fruit to the tea and put over a low heat for 10 minutes.

Place next eight ingredients in a large saucepan and bring to the boil. Simmer for 30 minutes.

Meanwhile, peel the pears and cut into quarters. Sprinkle with lemon juice, to prevent browning. Add the pears to the wine syrup and simmer until the pears are just cooked – about 10 minutes.

Drain the prunes and apricots, discarding the tea. Add to the pears. Cool, then refrigerate overnight.

....

NOTE: You can use fresh tamarillos in place of the pears. If using tamarillos, remove the skins by plunging into boiling water.

Steamed Golden Syrup Pudding

¹/₃ cup golden syrup
200 g softened butter
¹/₂ cup caster sugar
¹/₂ cup brown sugar
4 large eggs
1 teaspoon vanilla
1 teaspoon finely grated lemon rind
1¹/₂–1²/₃ cups flour
1¹/₄ teaspoons baking powder
4 tablespoons milk

Lightly grease and flour a 1.5 litre capacity pudding basin. Pour the golden syrup into the bottom of the basin.

Cream the butter and sugars until light and fluffy. Beat in the eggs one at a time, beating well after each addition. Add the vanilla and lemon rind and beat well. Sift the flour and baking powder and gently mix into the creamed mixture. Add the milk.

Pile the batter into the pudding basin, making sure the surface is level. Cover with a lid and steam for 1¹/₂ hours in a large pot half-filled with simmering water and sealed with a tight-fitting lid. Serve hot with custard and/or cream.

**Spiced Fruit
Compote**

Pumpkin and Date Cake

When we filled the airwaves with delicious recipes on a radio talkback show, a caller, Christine Perry, faxed in this great cake recipe – a family favourite for us all to enjoy. Yum!

250 g butter, softened
$3/4$ cup caster sugar
2 eggs
1 cup chopped dates
$1/2$ cup coconut
$1/2$ cup cold mashed pumpkin
1 tablespoon finely grated orange rind
2 cups self-raising flour
$1/2$ cup milk

Butter and line a 24 cm tin with baking paper. Cream the butter and sugar. Add the eggs. Stir in the dates, coconut, pumpkin and orange rind. Stir in half the flour and half the milk. Blend gently, then add the remaining flour and milk. Place in the cake pan and bake at 160°C. Check the cake after 60 minutes, or, for a fan bake oven, after 45 minutes.

Banana Coconut Pudding

Serves 4–6

100 g butter
1 cup brown sugar
3–4 bananas

TOPPING:
1 cup flour
$1/2$ cup coconut
2 teaspoons baking powder
$1/3$ cup sugar
pinch of salt
65 g butter
1 egg
$3/4$ cup milk

Melt the butter in an oven-proof dish. I like to use my glass lasagne baking dish (18 cm x 28 cm) for this recipe. Add the brown sugar and slice the bananas lengthwise and place on top of the melted butter and sugar.

Topping: Mix the dry ingredients together and work in the butter so the mixture is crumbly. Drop the egg into the milk. Mix well and add to the dry ingredients.

Place the topping on the bananas in the ovenproof dish and bake at 180°C for 35–45 minutes till the topping is golden brown.

NOTE: Squeeze a little fresh lemon juice over the bananas before placing the topping on the mix – it keeps the rich sweetness of the butter and sugar mix in balance with the rest of the flavours. Serve with cream or vanilla ice-cream or both.

Blackberry Cobbler

An American-inspired dessert to celebrate blackberries.

Serves 4

60 g butter
$^{1}/_{2}$ cup sugar
1 cup flour
2 teaspoons baking powder
$^{1}/_{4}$ teaspoon salt
$^{1}/_{2}$ cup milk
1–1$^{1}/_{2}$ cups blackberries
$^{1}/_{4}$ cup sugar
1 cup fruit juice or water

Beat the butter and the first measure of sugar together until well mixed. Sift together the flour, baking powder and salt. Stir into the creamed butter and sugar mix with the milk. Beat until smooth.

Pour into a buttered 20 cm x 20 cm ovenproof dish. Spoon the blackberries over the batter, then sprinkle the second measure of sugar over the top. Pour the fruit juice/water over the sugar and fruit.

Bake at 190°C for 35–45 minutes. Serve with vanilla ice-cream and/or cream.

Greek Orange Syrup Cake

This cake is a delight – make it and wait for the compliments!

5 eggs
1 cup caster sugar
zest and juice of 2 oranges
225 g butter, melted
1 cup flour
3 teaspoons baking powder

ORANGE GLAZE:
$^{1}/_{4}$ cup orange juice
$^{1}/_{4}$ cup sugar
2 tablespoons Grand Marnier

Butter and flour a 23 cm tin. Line the bottom with baking paper.

Separate the eggs. Cream the egg yolks and sugar. Add the orange zest and juice. Stir in the melted butter, then carefully fold in the sifted flour and baking powder.

Whisk the egg whites to a soft peak stage. Fold one tablespoon of the beaten egg whites into the cake mixture, then fold in the remaining egg whites.

Place in the prepared tin and bake in a 180°C oven for 35–40 minutes until golden and the sides of the cake begin to come away from the tin. Remove from the oven. Make a few holes in the top of the cake with a wooden skewer. Carefully spoon over the orange glaze.

Orange Glaze: Combine $^{1}/_{4}$ cup orange juice and $^{1}/_{4}$ cup sugar in a saucepan and simmer gently for 5 minutes, stirring occasionally, until a light syrup forms. Remove from the heat and add 2 tablespoons of Grand Marnier.

NOTE: This recipe doubles well. The cake will sink slightly in the middle and has the consistency of a baked cheese cake.

Pantry Classics

Everyone loves a pantry full of home-made treats.

Here are some of our favourite offerings.

Pickled Gherkins

5 kg small gherkins
1 cup salt
2 litres white vinegar
5 cups sugar
2 tablespoons pickling spice
1 stick cinnamon

Wash the gherkins thoroughly. Soak overnight in the salt and 2½ litres of water. Drain and rinse off excess salt, then pour over boiling water to cover.

Place the vinegar, sugar, spice and cinnamon in a saucepan. Dissolve the sugar and then allow to boil. Drain the gherkins and pack into hot jars. Cover with the boiling vinegar and seal using the overflow method and Agee seals.

Leave for one month before eating.

Cumberland Sauce with Dried Cranberries

4 tablespoons redcurrant jelly
2 glasses port
rind and juice of 2 oranges
juice of 1 lemon
½ cup dried cranberries

Heat the jelly in a saucepan until dissolved. Stir in the remaining ingredients. Serve with ham or at Christmas with your turkey.

....

NOTE: You can also make this recipe using sour cherries in place of the dried cranberries.

Bev's Best Jam

My mother, Bev, makes the best jam Annabelle or I have tasted. She makes small quantities, so it's always fresh. **KP**

berry fruit – raspberries, loganberries,
   boysenberries or tayberries
sugar – to every 500 g of berries allow
   500 g of sugar
butter

Put the fruit into a preserving pan and bring slowly to the boil. Add the sugar gradually and boil quickly for 5 minutes. Remove from the heat, add a knob of butter and stir for 20 minutes or until all sediment has been stirred in.

Put into warm, sterilised jars and seal with jam covers, and a screw-top if available.

Green Peppercorn Sauce

This sauce is delicious as an accompaniment to the Roasted Lamb Loin with Lemon Grass on pages 60/61.

250 ml chicken stock
30 g lemon grass, sliced
2 teaspoons root ginger, crushed
150 ml cream
2 teaspoons green peppercorns, crushed
knob of butter

Boil the chicken stock, lemon grass and ginger until reduced by half. Strain and then add the cream and peppercorns and continue to reduce until you have achieved the desired consistency and flavour.

Add the butter and stir well. This butter addition will give the sauce a glossy appearance.

Tamarillo Chutney

885 g or about 17 tamarillos

600 g or about 3 apples

445 g onions

2 cups vinegar

$3/4$ teaspoon cayenne pepper

1 tablespoon salt

2 cups raisins

1 tablespoon mixed spice

3 cups packed brown sugar

Scald and skin the tamarillos. Peel and core the apples. Peel the onions. Chop up the fruit and onions and place in a large preserving pan with all the other ingredients, keeping aside $1/2$ cup of the vinegar. Cook the chutney slowly, stirring regularly, until thick and dark, adding the last measure of vinegar after 60 minutes of cooking.

Pack into sterilised jars and store in a cool, dark place.

....

NOTE: For this chutney allow 4 hours in total for cooking time.

Shona's Pickled Plums

My mother has a great friend, Shona, who simply loves to get in a pickle. She searches cookbooks and magazines and even talks to growers about her favourite subject – making preserves. From pickled walnuts to pickled plums, Shona is the true pickle devotee. Nothing is safe from her pickling brine. The results are scrumptious! **AW**

600 ml white wine vinegar

12 black peppercorns

1 teaspoon whole cloves

4 cardamom pods

2 cinnamon sticks

2 star anise

1 kg sugar

2 kg dark red plums, halved

Bring the vinegar and spices to a boil and add the sugar. Turn the heat to low, until the sugar is completely dissolved. Boil gently for 2 minutes. Add the halved plums and simmer for 4–5 minutes.

Bottle but do not seal.

Red Onion Marmalade

This recipe has endless possibilities. Serve it warm as a sauce over chicken, or chilled, paired with cream cheese, on top of a toasted onion bagel.

Makes 3–4 cups

1 tablespoon olive oil

3 medium red onions, finely chopped

2 jalapeño or other hot chilli peppers, seeded and minced

$1/4$ cup dry-packed sun-dried tomatoes, minced

1 tart cooking apple such as Granny Smith, quartered, cored, peeled and grated

$1/2$ cup sultanas

$3/4$ cup red wine vinegar

1 cup firmly packed brown sugar

1 cinnamon stick

1 cup apple juice or water

salt, to taste

Warm the oil in a large, heavy-bottomed saucepan over medium-low heat. Add the onions and chillies and cook for approximately 10–15 minutes, or until the onions are soft.

Add all the remaining ingredients except the salt. Place over a low heat and bring to a gentle simmer. Cook, uncovered, for approximately 1 hour, or until all the ingredients are soft and the marmalade begins to thicken. Stir frequently. If all the moisture has evaporated but the onions aren't fully cooked, add more water and continue to cook until the mixture is reduced to a thick, jam-like consistency.

Remove from the heat. Season with salt and remove the cinnamon stick. You may choose to add more chilli pepper at this time. Store in the refrigerator for up to two weeks.

....

NOTE: This marmalade is delicious with roast chicken or pan-fried chicken and served with a bed of mashed potatoes and swedes. Boil the vegetables separately and then mash together with a generous knob of butter. Season before serving.

Acknowledgements

We travelled to Queenstown in the South Island to capture the essence of the enchanting Evergreen Lodge for this cookbook. A huge thanks to the lodge's stylist, John Borwick, for making it all possible. His enthusiasm and energy to find the right location and help create our dream settings was tremendous.

Thanks also to the team that helped make all our ideas and shared vision a reality: food stylist Rodney Greaves, recipe tester and stylist Nicola Muir, recipe tester Penny Pearson, stylist Lynley Snell, book designer Sue Attwood, photographer Kieran Scott, editor Margaret Sinclair and to Belinda Cooke, Renée Lang and all the New Holland team – thank you for your support.

Many thanks to Gourmet Direct, in particular Jenny Myers, for her expert guidance and support in sourcing and sending us the best possible products for our photography.
Thanks also to Air New Zealand, Matua Wines, Chubby Chicken, The BBQ Factory and the Studio of Tableware in Mt Eden for the use of their stunning cake stand on page 69 and the glassware on page 91.

A special thanks to Karin Crawley of Imagetext for supplying a replacement computer two weeks before deadline, when the one with all the recipes became inoperative. Also a huge thank you to Genevieve Westcott for all her support and assistance.

Special thanks to our friends and families who supported us in this venture, and to all the 'samplers' far and wide who enthused and were so positive – we couldn't have completed this book without your enjoyment. Your requests for recipes pre-publication have been encouraging.

At the end of a long day, when the dishes have piled up in the sink, and you've been frantically busy styling food, fossicking around in a sea of cupboards for a certain plate or glass, not to mention testing recipes and double-checking cake tin sizes, you need the humour and affection good friendship brings ... so to all those who wish to remain anonymous – thank you.

Weights and Measures

As most cooks do not have scales in their kitchen,
where possible we have indicated measurements in cups and tablespoons.
Cup measures are loosely filled except for brown sugar, which is firmly packed.
Butter is presented in grams.

In New Zealand, South Africa, the USA and in England
1 tablespoon equals 15 ml. In Australia, 1 tablespoon equals 20 ml.
These variations will not adversely affect the end result, as long as the same spoon
is used consistently, so the proportions are correct.

Grams to Ounces and vice versa

General	Exact
30 g = 1 oz	1 oz = 28.35 g
60 g = 2 oz	2 oz = 56.70 g
90 g = 3 oz	3 oz = 85.05 g
120 g = 4 oz	4 oz = 113.04 g
150 g = 5 oz	5 oz = 141.08 g
180 g = 6 oz	6 oz = 170.01 g
210 g = 7 oz	7 oz = 198.04g
230 g = 8 oz	8 oz = 226.08 g
260 g = 9 oz	9 oz = 255.01 g
290 g = 10 oz	10 oz = 283.05 g
320 g = 11 oz	11 oz = 311.08 g
350 g = 12 oz	12 oz = 340.02 g
380 g = 13 oz	13 oz = 368.05 g
410 g = 14 oz	14 oz = 396.09 g
440 g = 15 oz	15 oz = 425.02 g
470 g = 16 oz	16 oz = 453.06 g

Recipes based on these (International Units) rounded values

Liquid Measurements

25 ml	(28.4 ml)	=1 fl oz		
150 ml	(142 ml)	=5 fl oz	= $\frac{1}{4}$ pint	= 1 gill
275 ml	(284 ml)	=10 fl oz	= $\frac{1}{2}$ pint	
425 ml	(426 ml)	=15 f1 oz	= $\frac{3}{4}$ pint	
575 ml	(568 ml)	=20 fl oz	= 1 pint	

Spoon Measures

$\frac{1}{4}$ teaspoon = 1.25 ml
$\frac{1}{2}$ teaspoon = 2.5 ml
1 teaspoon = 5 ml
1 tablespoon = 15 ml

In NZ, SA, USA and UK 1 tablespoon = 15ml.
In Australia 1 tablespoon = 20ml.

Measurements
cm to approx inches

0.5 cm = $\frac{1}{4}$"		5 cm = 2"	
1.25 cm = $\frac{1}{2}$"		7.5 cm = 3"	
2.5 cm = 1"		10 cm = 4"	

Cake Tin Sizes
cm to approx inches

15 cm = 6 "	23 cm = 9 "
18 cm = 7 "	25 cm = 10 "
20 cm = 8 "	

Alternative Names

cake tin	cake/baking pan
capsicum	sweet bell pepper
coriander	cilantro
cornflour	cornstarch
eggplant	aubergine
essence	extract
frypan	skillet
grill	broil
hard-boiled egg	hard-cooked egg
icing sugar	confectioner's sugar
king prawns	jumbo shrimps/scampi
kumara	sweet potato
minced meat	ground meat
pawpaw	papaya
rock melon	cantaloupe
seed	pip
spring onion	scallion/green onion
zucchini	courgette

Oven Temperatures
Celsius to Fahrenheit

110°C	225°F	very cool
130°C	250°F	
140°C	275°F	cool
150°C	300°F	
170°C	325°F	warm
180°C	350°F	moderate
190°C	375°F	fairly hot
200°C	400°F	
220°C	425°F	hot
230°C	450°F	very hot
240°C	475°F	

Abbreviations / American-Imperial

g	grams		in	inch
kg	kilogram		lb	pound
mm	millimetre		oz	ounce
cm	centimetre			
ml	millilitre			
°C	degrees celsius			
°F	degrees Farenheit			

Index

Index